# Scripting Junior

**Social Skill Role-Plays**

**Elementary**

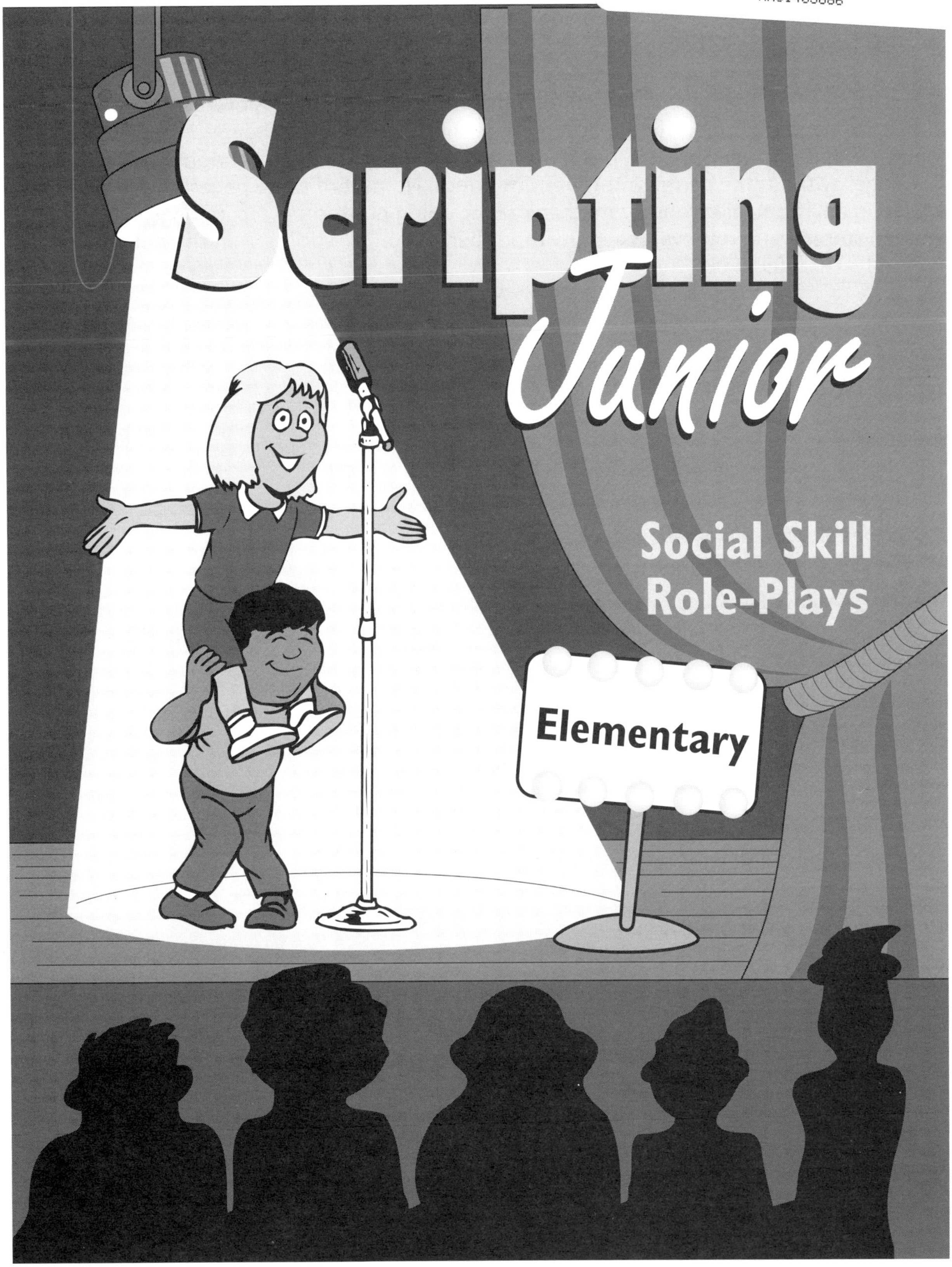

Lynda Miller

Super Duper® Publications • Greenville, South Carolina

© 2007 by Super Duper® Publications
© 2004 by Thinking Publications®

Super Duper® Publications grants limited rights to individual professionals to reproduce and distribute pages that indicate duplication is permissible. Pages can be used for instruction only and must include Super Duper® Publications' copyright notice. All rights are reserved for pages without the permission-to-reprint notice. No part of these pages can be reproduced in any form, electronic or mechanical, including photocopy, recording, or any information storage and retrieval system, without permission in writing from the publisher.

12 11 10 09 08                                                8 7 6 5 4 3 2

*Library of Congress Cataloging-in-Publication Data*

Miller, Lynda.
   Scripting junior : social skill role-plays : elementary / Lynda Miller.
     p. cm.
   Includes bibliographical references.
   ISBN 978-1-932054-22-7 (pbk.)
    1. Social skills—Study and teaching (Elementary). 2. Social skills—Study and teaching (Elementary)—Activity programs. 3. Social skills in children. 4. Role playing. I. Title.

HQ783.M56 2004
372.82—dc22

2004051760

*Printed in the United States of America*

*Cover design by Debbie Olson*

**Trademarks:** All brand names and product names used in this book are trade names,
          service marks,
            trademarks, or registered trademarks of their respective owners.

Super Duper® Publications
Post Office Box 24997, Greenville, South Carolina 29616
www.superduperinc.com • 1-800-277-8737 • Fax 1-800-978-7379

To my family and friends,
all of whom have inspired and supported me
in ways too numerous to recount.

# About the Author

Lynda Miller, PhD, has devoted her career to the development and dissemination of innovative ideas in learning and communication. For over 30 years, Lynda has studied education and the most effective practices for enhancing students' learning. She writes and edits books and materials on narrative, learning, intelligence, communication, and school-related issues. Lynda has worked as a speech-language clinician and developmental learning specialist with children and adults of all ages. She has taught at universities and colleges in Colorado, Montana, Illinois, and Texas.

Currently, Lynda writes books and materials for teachers and other educational professionals, and she designs and writes online continuing education courses for professionals meeting licensure requirements. In addition, Lynda does graphic design for children's books and print advertising, and she designs and builds websites for a variety of clients.

# Contents

**Preface** ...................................................................................................................... vii

**Acknowledgments** ...................................................................................................... viii

## Chapter 1: Introduction ........................................................................................... 1
    Overview .............................................................................................................. 1
    Description of *Scripting Junior* ............................................................................ 4
    How to Use *Scripting Junior* ............................................................................... 7

## Chapter 2: Skill Step Presentation ........................................................................... 9
    Step 1: Identification of the Problem .................................................................... 9
    Step 2: Identification of the Skill .......................................................................... 9
    Step 3: Introduction of the Skill .......................................................................... 10
    Step 4: Skill Presentation .................................................................................... 11
    Step 5: Scripting ................................................................................................. 12
    Step 6: Using Alternative Settings ....................................................................... 12
    Step 7: Skill Role-Play ......................................................................................... 12
    Step 8: Follow-Up Activities ................................................................................ 13
    Step 9: Concluding Activities .............................................................................. 13
    Step 10: Review and Reinforcement .................................................................... 13
    Summary ............................................................................................................ 13

## Social Communication Skills Scripts ...................................................................... 15
### General Interaction Skills ....................................................................................... 16
    Skill 1: Cognitive Planning .................................................................................. 16
    Skill 2: Eye Contact ............................................................................................ 20
    Skill 3: Volume ................................................................................................... 24
    Skill 4: Tone of Voice ......................................................................................... 28
    Skill 5: Facial Expression .................................................................................... 32
    Skill 6: Posture ................................................................................................... 36
    Skill 7: Personal Space ........................................................................................ 40
    Skill 8: Hygiene .................................................................................................. 44
    Skill 9: Body Talk ............................................................................................... 48
    Skill 10: Manners ............................................................................................... 52

## Contents

    Skill 11: Listening Basics ..................................................................................56
    Skill 12: Staying On and Switching Topics .....................................................60
    Skill 13: Conversations ....................................................................................64
    Skill 14: Interrupting........................................................................................68
    Skill 15: Right Time and Place .........................................................................72
    Skill 16: Being Formal or Casual .....................................................................76

**Peer Interaction Skills** ..........................................................................................80
    Skill 17: Optimism ..........................................................................................80
    Skill 18: Playing Cooperatively .......................................................................86
    Skill 19: Respecting Differences .....................................................................92
    Skill 20: Being a Friend ...................................................................................99
    Skill 21: Giving & Receiving a Compliment ................................................106
    Skill 22: Building a Positive Reputation.......................................................112
    Skill 23: Dealing with Teasing......................................................................119
    Skill 24: Getting into a Group ......................................................................126
    Skill 25: Giving Put-Ups ................................................................................133
    Skill 26: Participating ...................................................................................140
    Skill 27: Staying on Task ...............................................................................147
    Skill 28: Disagreeing Politely ........................................................................154

**Conflict Resolution and Community Interaction Skills** ...................................161
    Skill 29: Taking Charge of Feelings ..............................................................161
    Skill 30 Being Assertive ................................................................................168
    Skill 31: Being Responsible ..........................................................................174
    Skill 32: Taking Charge of Anger ..................................................................181
    Skill 33: Resisting Peer Pressure ..................................................................188
    Skill 34: Settling Conflicts............................................................................195
    Skill 35: Making an Apology.........................................................................202
    Skill 36: Responding to Criticism .................................................................209
    Skill 37: Helping My Community .................................................................216

**Appendix: Follow-Up Activities** .........................................................................223

**References**..........................................................................................................229

# Preface

*Scripting Junior: Social Skill Role-Plays* guides educators in teaching their students the social communication skills needed to succeed in school and to participate more successfully at home and in their communities. *Scripting Junior* owes a tremendous debt to its predecessor, *Scripting: Social Communication for Adolescents* (Mayo & Waldo, 1994) and its authors, Patty Mayo and Pattii Waldo, who originated the idea of integrating the skill-step approach with a scripting technique.

Mayo and Waldo, professionals working in the classroom, designed their scripts for adolescent students. Their work evolved out of their belief that students with social disabilities struggle when they encounter social situations requiring knowledge about how to act, what to say, and how to evaluate what is happening.

*Scripting Junior* is shaped around Mayo and Waldo's successful model for teaching social skills. The scripts are written at or below the fourth grade level per the Flesch-Kincaid readability formula, which permits the program to be used with students of varying reading abilities. Many of the scripts contain characters who speak only a few words or lines, thus enabling students to memorize, rather than read, their parts. The scripted activities used in *Scripting Junior* provide the structure needed for students who may have attention deficits or minimal self-control.

Because social competence contributes considerably to students' academic success (Paul, 2001; Polloway, Miller, & Smith, 2004), the activities in *Scripting Junior* are designed to help students increase both academic and social competence. Through the direct instruction incorporated into *Scripting Junior,* educators help students develop the abilities necessary for participation in the wide range of social situations students experience in their everyday lives.

# Acknowledgments

I owe a considerable debt to several people who, directly or indirectly, contributed to the design and completion of this project.

To Nancy McKinley, thank you for providing me the opportunity to work on *Scripting Junior: Social Skill Role-Plays*. I've had great fun conjuring scenarios that would be both fun and instructive for elementary school students. I am appreciative of your humor, generosity, and good cheer—all of which permeate this endeavor.

To Vicki Lord Larson, thank you for your thoughtful guidance, particularly at the outset, when I pestered you with numerous questions and requests for clarifications. I am grateful for the expertise and knowledge you shared with me.

To Linda Schreiber and Vicki Fields, much appreciation for your thoughtfulness in shaping the final version of this book. I'm especially grateful for your creative ideas for incorporating the reviewers' constructive and practical comments.

To the field reviewers, Polly Hirn, a big thank-you for the care you took in testing the scripts with your students. Your insights, suggestions, and recommendations have greatly enhanced this book.

To Patty Mayo and Pattii Waldo, your text, *Scripting: Social Communication for Adolescents* served as a stellar template for this book. Because your approach continues to be relevant, pertinent, and dedicated to helping students experience more success and less failure, I incorporated as much of it as possible into this book. Thanks for being such great forerunners.

To Lynn Miller, thank you for your expert review of the scripts. Although the students using this book won't know it, you saved them from a few wild scenarios and more than one ponderous sentence.

# Chapter 1
# Introduction

## Overview

*Mr. Wall is assigning his students to learning groups for their first project of the school year. A few students appear hesitant to join their groups. Two students in one of the groups are arguing over how the group should proceed—using loud voices to give put-downs. Mr. Wall observes another group in which the students are sitting slumped and looking down silently at their notebooks.*

*As Mr. Wall begins to give his instructions to the students, one student jumps out of his chair and starts toward the pencil sharpener. He intentionally bumps into the back of another student, jostling his arm so his pencil rips his paper.*

Elementary school teachers regularly observe behaviors that interfere with students' ability to interact with each other and to learn in the social setting of the classroom. Students displaying many of these behaviors can be described as having a social skill deficit that interferes with their ability to maintain social acceptance by peers and adults. Students of all abilities in the elementary grade levels can benefit from added practice in social communication skills. *Scripting Junior: Social Skill Role-Plays* is designed to be used by teachers with students in grades 2 through 5 who, like

# Scripting Junior

the students in Mr. Wall's class, are socially different (i.e., unable to maintain social acceptance by peers and adults [Mayo & Waldo, 1994]) or who have a social skill deficit. Elliott and Gresham (1991) proposed five reasons why a student may have a social skill deficit:

1. Lack of knowledge
2. Lack of practice or feedback
3. Lack of cues or opportunities
4. Lack of reinforcement
5. Presence of interfering behaviors

Skill with social language, also known as pragmatics, contributes to students' academic progress and success (Polloway, Miller, & Smith, 2004). Conversely, a social skill deficit can inhibit students' learning and academic achievement. Acquiring the specific social skills necessary to cope with the demands of the regular classroom will help to ensure that students experience success in the classroom and transfer this learning to other areas of their lives.

Classroom teachers can easily identify students who require social skill training. Providing these students with appropriate classroom experiences often demands a careful and sustained approach that goes beyond simply mainstreaming them in the hope that they will benefit socially through incidental social learning. In fact, it appears that, for students with social skill deficits, classroom social interaction and social acceptance do not occur unless they are provided specific training in social skills.

A variety of approaches has been used with students demonstrating social differences and deficits. Madden and Slavin (1983) describe six methods:

1. Coaching
2. Teaching the skills
3. Providing feedback
4. Modeling
5. Using behavior modification
6. Learning cooperatively

Strain, Odom, and McConnell (1984) discuss a skill training model that involves:

- Modeling the skill for students
- Having students role-play skills
- Reinforcing the skill
- Initiating skills by peers

Using a structured learning approach is advocated in McGinnis, Goldstein, Sprafkin, and Gershaw (1984), and in Goldstein, Sprafkin, Gershaw, and Klein (1980). McGinnis et al. (1984) describe a structured learning approach as "a psychoeducational intervention designed to teach the skill deficient child prosocial behaviors and to facilitate the actual use of these alternatives" (p. 8). The structured learning approach utilizes the following four training components which were used as the basis for *Scripting Junior: Social Skill Role-Plays:*

1. Modeling
2. Role-playing
3. Performance feedback
4. Transfer of training

*Scripting Junior* offers a structured approach to the practice of social communication skills that utilizes the types of everyday situations typical of elementary school students. Taken together, the scripts, situations, and activities can be used as a unit approach to teaching social skills. Through learning and practicing appropriate social communication skills, students can develop the social skill competence required to succeed not only in the classroom, but also in their everyday lives outside of school.

*Scripting Junior* follows the same format used in *Scripting: Social Communication for Adolescents* (Mayo & Waldo, 1994), which was originally developed within a public school program for adolescents with behavioral disorders. Mayo and Waldo designed their scripts to be used with students with learning disabilities, language disabilities, and cognitive impairments. Their scripts were also tested on general education junior high school students who needed social skill training. Those scripts that proved effective were ultimately incorporated into *Scripting: Social Communication for Adolescents.*

*Scripting Junior* is designed to be used as a companion to the *Social Star* series—a comprehensive, experiential curriculum that teaches elementary school students appropriate social skills—which includes:

- *Social Star: General Interaction Skills (Book 1)* (Gajewski, Hirn, & Mayo, 1993)
- *Social Star: Peer Interaction Skills (Book 2)* (Gajewski, Hirn, & Mayo, 1994)
- *Social Star: Conflict Resolution and Community Interaction Skills (Book 3)* (Gajewski, Hirn, & Mayo, 1996)

*Scripting Junior* provides scripts to accompany each of the social skills taught in the *Social Star* Series. For *Social Star: General Interaction Skills (Book 1)*, there is one *Scripting Junior* script to illustrate the appropriate use of each of the general interaction skills included. For *Social Star: Peer Interaction Skills (Book 2)* and *Social Star: Conflict Resolution and Community Interaction Skills (Book 3)*, there are two *Scripting Junior* scripts—Script A and Script B—for each skill. Each Script A demonstrates an appropriate way to use the skill, while each Script B demonstrates an inappropriate way, providing students with an example of what happens when a skill is lacking or is used inappropriately.

# Scripting Junior

The scripts in *Scripting Junior: Social Skill Role-Plays* have readability levels (as measured by Flesch-Kincaid grade levels) ranging from 0.2 to 4.2—the majority being below 3.5. Teachers can include low-level or non-readers by recording their parts aloud for them ahead of time so they can listen to the recordings in order to memorize their lines and actions. Alternatively, the teacher can draw (or have the students draw) simple pictograms to represent actions or lines of the script so that low-level or non-readers can use them to identify when their parts arise and what they're supposed to say and do. Teachers making these modifications for students should read the scripts well before presenting them to the class so that they can make the most appropriate modifications for each script.

Although *Scripting Junior* is designed to compliment the *Social Star* series, it can also be used as a stand-alone program providing the structured approach advocated by McGinnis et al. (1984) and including activities, situations, and scripts that form the basis for specific skill units. The situations were selected from real-life experiences of elementary school students in a variety of situations (i.e., home, school, and community). The situations provided in the scripts and discussions can be used by the students for practicing specific social skills. The scripts themselves offer a means to introduce or reinforce specific social skills during role-playing experiences.

# Description of *Scripting Junior*

## Skill Steps

Each skill step breaks down the social skill into specific consecutive instructions which lead to the completion of the skill. This process is similar to a task analysis, in which the target skill is identified and then broken down into teachable units of behavior. Skill steps are used in the *Social Star* series, where the skill is introduced, skill steps are presented, and students then discuss each step and compare the steps with previously learned skills or arrange the steps in appropriate order. The cognitive planning strategy in *Scripting Junior* is an offshoot of "Stop, Plot, Go, So," a strategy introduced in *Social Star (Book I)*, to analyze behavior and its consequences. If *Scripting Junior* is being used as a complement to the *Social Star* series, the "Stop, Plot, Go, So" terms and icons can replace the terms "Calm Down, Think, Act, Then What?" (which are used in *Scripting Junior*) in teaching the cognitive planning strategy.

## Staging

Staging includes instructions and notes to the educator, with a definition of the skill, activities and discussion ideas to elaborate on the skills use, and three alternative setups in which to apply the skill.

## Alternative Settings

Following the model used in *Scripting: Social Communication for Adolescents,* three situations are presented in the Alternative Settings section of each skill unit: one from a home setting, one from a school setting, and one from a community setting. According to Mayo and Waldo (1994), these environments were selected to:

- "Illustrate the relevance of the skill within the students' lives;
- Promote transfer of the skill from the classroom into other environments; and
- Increase the students' experiences with the skill" (p. 6).

These situations can be used for role playing after the students have read and performed the scripts. The staging page may be duplicated, and the alternative settings section may be used as a student handout.

## Scripts

After the students are familiar with a particular skill, one of the scripts from *Scripting Junior* can be read. The description of each scene orients the students to the scene and affords them an opportunity to choose the parts they prefer. Rather than having students select the parts, teachers may decide when it would be better to assign parts themselves.

Although each character has been assigned a name, students may wish to cross out the fictional name and write in their own. If the students require additional practice, they can break the monotony of rereading the script by creating their own fictional names. The names used in the scripts are intended to reflect the various cultures represented in U.S. classrooms. However, if students experience difficulty in pronouncing the names, teachers might want to conduct a discussion about how names vary across cultural groups or about how names don't necessarily indicate inherent qualities in a person.

The scripts in *Scripting Junior* are reproducible. To individualize the experience, the educator can customize the scripts for each student's particular needs. For instance, the educator can color-code the script for students who have difficulty following the narrative. If students have difficulty with reading, the educator can provide individual assistance to help students follow the scripts. In addition, students who have difficulty reading can practice the script during class or at home before reading them in class. In some of the scripts the characters each say only a few words, making it easier for students to memorize the lines rather than read them.

# Scripting Junior

The scripts can be used by large or small groups. In large groups, some students can be assigned parts, while the others listen. Also, the part of the narrator (the one who reads all the information in the brackets) can be assigned. When students are using the scripts in large groups, the observers should be given specific instructions (e.g., "listen for the skill steps," or "identify how the problem in this situation was solved.")

If there are more characters than students, each student can take more than one role and change their voice, gestures, posture, and facial expressions to represent each character. The educator should read the scripts ahead of time to determine which combinations of characters would be suitable for students to read.

As described earlier, for *Social Star: Peer Interaction Skills (Book 2),* and *Social Star: Conflict Resolution and Community Interaction Skills (Book 3),* two *Scripting Junior* scripts are provided in each skill unit. Depending on the needs of the group, one or both scripts may be chosen for use within the skill unit.

Script A is used to reinforce the skill steps in a practical situation. It illustrates the correct performance of the skill and offers students the opportunity to practice the skill appropriately. Students can be asked to describe other situations from their own lives in which this skill can be used.

Script B demonstrates the skill being used inappropriately and provides a way for students to see what goes wrong when the skill is not used. After going through Script B, the educator can encourage the students to discuss the skill steps that were not followed, to suggest more appropriate ways of reacting to the situation described in the script, or to describe what happened when they were in the same or a similar situation. The primary objective of using Script B is to discuss what went wrong in the script and what might have happened if the skill had been demonstrated appropriately. Another way in which to use Script B is for teachers to help their students rewrite the inappropriate scripts so that they reflect the skill being used appropriately.

## Follow-Up Activities

The follow-up activities, or homework experiences, were designed to promote skill transfer and generalization. After the students have demonstrated understanding of the skill through discussions, script readings, and role-playing, the follow-up activities provide a way for the students to practice the skill in their own environment, ideally outside the classroom. Four Follow-Up Activity templates are provided in the Appendix (pages 223–228). Select the sheet corresponding to the experiences you determine is the best for the student(s), and customize accordingly.

# How to Use *Scripting Junior*

Each skill unit has been designed to take approximately 30 to 40 minutes a day over a four- or five-day period. However, the length of each skill unit can be adjusted based on students' abilities and needs. Mayo and Waldo (1994) suggested breaking the five days into segments. *Scripting Junior* recommends a similar schedule, as below:

**Day One:** Introduce the skill.
**Day Two:** Present the skill.
**Day Three:** Present the script.
**Day Four:** Model and role-play the skill, critique the role-playing, and provide a homework assignment.
**Day Five:** Conduct concluding discussions, and review the homework experiences.

The scripts provided in *Scripting Junior* are in the developmental order utilized in the *Social Star* series. *General Interaction Skills (Book 1)* should be studied first, followed by *Peer Interaction Skills (Book 2)* and then by *Conflict Resolution and Community Involvement Skills (Book 3)*. The first 16 scripts correspond to General Interaction Skills. The skills learned in these scripts are a foundation to the other skills and should be constantly reinforced throughout the skill training program. For instance, when conducting Skill 22, "Building a Positive Reputation," emphasize the importance of "Eye Contact" (Skill 2) and "Tone of Voice" (Skill 4). Ask students to recall what they learned about eye contact and tone of voice so they can incorporate those skills as they practice the scripts for "Building a Positive Reputation" (Skill 22). Or, ask students to sketch the visual repesentation for skills in the margins of the script for reinforcement and review.

Mayo and Waldo (1994) believe that, to maintain student motivation, the skill activities "should be relevant to the students' experiences, needs, and interests" (p. 7). *Scripting Junior* offers situations and scripts that correspond to the everyday lives of elementary school children, such as:

- Home and family
- School
- Peers
- Community awareness

Among the means to enhance motivation described by Mayo and Waldo (1994) are the use of humor and laughter, and community field trips where students can practice their skills (e.g., restaurants, museums, libraries, newspapers, television stations). Mayo and Waldo (1994) also recommend encouraging students to share their personal experiences in order to make the skill units more interesting and relevant. In addition, they point out that such personal sharing also highlights cultural and regional differences for each skill.

# Scripting Junior

When social skill training is integrated into the students' day, *Scripting Junior* can be used to enhance the students' abilities in various content areas, particularly reading, language arts, and English. The scripts can be used to help students improve reading fluency and expression, narrative language abilities, and written expression.

# Chapter 2
# Skill Step Presentation

*"That's my pencil, you thief!"*
*"Your hair looks weird."*
*"Give me that book, you jerk."*

*Mr. Wall listened to his students together in their small groups and was concerned that they weren't getting along with each other. The students didn't seem to know how to be nice to one another or how to change the way they talked to each other. He decided to do something about it.*

The following is an example of how Mr. Wall used *Scripting Junior* to solve the problems he saw occurring in his class through presenting social skill training.

## Step 1: Identification of the Problem

Mr. Wall was concerned that his students weren't getting along with each other. They spent more time putting each other down than productively working on their group assignment.

## Step 2: Identification of the Skill

Mr. Wall observed that many of his students acted impulsively and weren't thinking through their behavior and its consequences before, during, and after initiation. He decided to teach the skill of *cognitive planning*.

Scripting Junior

# Step 3: Introduction of the Skill

Mr. Wall posted the following on the board and on an overhead:

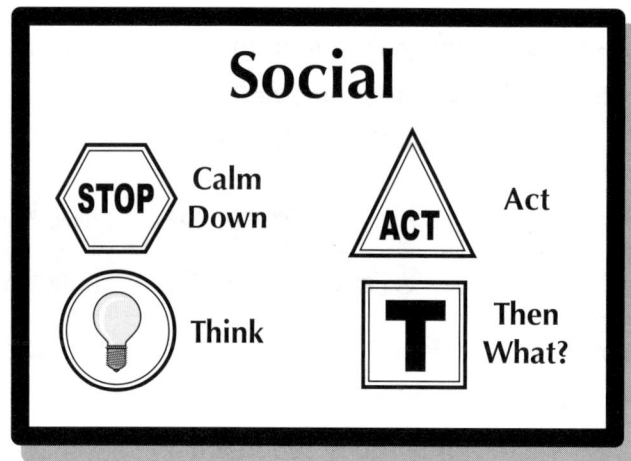

After the students were seated, he read the first line, **Social,** and asked the students what they thought it meant. He told them that the Merriam-Webster Online Dictionary defined *social* this way: "Marked by or passed in pleasant companionship with one's friends or associates" (2003). For students, this means "getting along with other people."

Mr. Wall directed the students in a discussion of what it means to share "pleasant companionship" with their friends and asked them for examples they had observed or experienced. Some students were able to give examples. For instance, Angela told Yolanda about a movie she'd seen, and Yolanda told Angela about the book she was reading. However, many of the students either could not think of examples, or they said things such as, "Marty told David his shoes were weird."

Next Mr. Wall pointed to each icon and discussed what they meant. He then asked the students to give examples of when they, or someone they had observed:

- Calmed down before saying something inappropriate

- Thought through what they wanted to say before saying it

- Acted using a response they thought would work best

- Then evaluated what happened by asking themselves, "So, what happened? Did my plan work? If not, why not and what can I do next time to make the plan work better?"

10

Although most students said they had used one of the behaviors they were discussing, almost none said they had ever used them all. Mr. Wall said, "It's important to be able to plan what you're going to say, and to think through what might happen when you say different things. This is called 'Cognitive Planning.' It's also important to know the difference between saying and doing. That's why we're going to be studying how to plan what we say and do and how it affects others."

## Step 4: Skill Presentation

In order to develop the steps involved in cognitive planning, Mr. Wall considered the cognitive planning behaviors of his students. As a result, he formulated these problem-solving ideas:

- Decide when I'm having trouble getting along with others. Ask myself, "Do I get angry and say things without thinking? Do I say things that make other people angry or upset? Do I get other people in trouble because of things I say?"

- Choose a situation where someone says or does something that makes me want to say something back to them without thinking.

- Try these four strategies:

     Calm down

     Think—Identify the problem and how to solve it

     Act—Decide how to act next

     Then what?—Ask myself what happened after I acted

During the second day of the unit, Mr. Wall presented the problem-solving ideas to the class and led them in a discussion of what each step meant. After the discussion, the students broke into pairs and brainstormed examples of each skill step. Finally, each pair presented their ideas to the whole class.

Scripting Junior

## Step 5: Scripting

After the students understood the skill steps, Mr. Wall presented the script from *Scripting Junior* to the class. He handed out printed copies to each student (including those with less developed reading skills). First, he read the script aloud; then he asked students to retell the script, guiding them in their retelling so they included the relevant parts. Next, he had the students select parts, and read or retell the script The students used simple props that added to the scene. Students who did not have a part were instructed to listen and to be ready to identify which part of the script showed each cognitive planning strategy. Mr. Wall suggested that the students draw the icons for the strategies in the margins of the script to help them remember.

After the students finished reading/retelling the script, Mr. Wall conducted a discussion summarizing the skill steps and how they showed up in the script. Throughout the discussion, Mr. Wall encouraged the students to share their own experiences and observations of using cognitive planning to get along with others.

## Step 6: Using Alternative Settings

Mr. Wall showed an overhead describing a situation that would likely be difficult for his students. He asked for a volunteer to help him role-play using cognitive planning and following all of the skill steps for the situation.

Mr. Wall and the volunteer rehearsed the skill steps, soliciting feedback from the other students, and then they role-played the situation, using all the skill steps. After the role-play, Mr. Wall conducted a class discussion to identify which parts of the role-play illustrated each skill step. Then he had students break into pairs and gave them three situations to practice. As they practiced, Mr. Wall visited each group to provide feedback and reinforce their efforts.

## Step 7: Skill Role-Play

By the time class ended, each student had an opportunity to practice the skill of *using cognitive planning* in a variety of situations. Mr. Wall asked each student to write down, or dictate, situations they could imagine in which it was necessary to use cognitive planning. During the next class period, they would present their own situation to the class in a role-play.

Mr. Wall made positive comments as the students presented their role-plays. Afterward, he reinforced the skill steps by mentioning the steps included in each.

## Step 8: Follow-Up Activities

After it appeared that the students had made progress with cognitive planning, he gave them the following homework assignment.

Practice using cognitive planning with a family member or friend. Write or dictate:
a. The skill steps
b. With whom you used cognitive planning
c. The situation in which you used cognitive planning

The person with whom the students used cognitive planning was asked to sign the follow-up activity sheet. In addition, Mr. Wall asked the students to keep a "cognitive planning" diary for one week and to record or dictate the situations in which they used cognitive planning. Mr. Wall discussed the diary each day with the students and provided time for students to practice together at various times throughout the week.

## Step 9: Concluding Activities

On the last day of the unit, Mr. Wall provided paints, markers, paper, pencils, and charcoal for the students. He asked the students to draw something representing each of the skill steps in cognitive planning. After the students were finished with their drawings, he asked the students to show them to the class and explain what they meant.

## Step 10: Review and Reinforcement

In the weeks following the presentation of the cognitive planning unit, Mr. Wall recognized and reinforced his students' use of the steps involved in cognitive planning. Occasionally, he provided students with opportunities to use cognitive planning by structuring specific situations.

## Summary

The 10 steps presented in developing a skill unit are intended as an example. The unit used in the example was simplified and did not include strategies or procedures to use when unexpected situations arise. Because each class has its own unique character, use creativity and judgment to determine whether to provide additional scripting or modeling examples, develop other strategies students can use, or

# Scripting Junior

modify the scripts and skill steps to accommodate students with particular needs. In-school practice and opportunities may be needed for students without adequate out-of-school resources.

Older elementary students may be skeptical about trying social skills training, and about using role-playing as a way to practice social skills. For these students, gradually introduce the process by structuring group activities that facilitate communication with peers. As students become more familiar with how such a group process works, they are more likely to engage in the actual training.

During the training, provide ongoing positive feedback to students. Give students exhibiting difficulty with self-control the job of providing a refreshment period at the end of class, contingent on their behavior and the completion of the assignment. Alternatively, issue grades for homework and for role-plays. However, before issuing grades for any given skill, first determine that the student can demonstrate skill mastery.

To ensure that follow-up activities are completed, enlist parents in the social skills training. Inform parents about the purpose and expected outcomes of social skills training. Meet informally with parents to convey this information, or send explanatory letters home. If parents are unable to work with their children, the students can practice new skills with a teacher, friend, or another adult outside the classroom.

Combined with other activities such as those in *Social Star*, the *Scripting Junior* program provides a comprehensive social skills program. *Scripting Junior: Social Skill Role-Plays* provides students with opportunities to develop awareness of social skills, how to use them appropriately, and how some people use them inappropriately. From activities, discussions, role-playing, and real-life practice, students experience situations that prepare them for successful social communication in their everyday lives.

*Social Communication*
# Skills Scripts

**General Interaction Skills** ............................................................................ 16

**Peer Interaction Skills** ................................................................................. 80

**Conflict Resolution and Community Interaction Skills** ........................ 161

— Skill 1 —

# Cognitive Planning

### Definition
Thinking about your behavior and its consequences before, during, and after you act or speak.

### Activities/Discussions

1. Discuss why it's important to think about behavior. Reasons might include preventing fights, communicating clearly, learning self-control, or getting along with others.

2. Discuss the consequences of not being able to think about their behavior. Ask them for examples.

3. Post these phrases and icons on an overhead or the board:

   **Social**

   Ask students what they think **Social** means. Ask the students to give examples of when they or someone they observed:

   - Calmed down before saying something inappropriate
   - Thought through what they wanted to say before saying it
   - Acted using a response they thought would work best
   - Then asked, "What happened? Did my plan work? If not, why not? What can I do next time to make the plan work better?"

4. Role-play two short examples of thinking about behavior. Discuss the examples.

## Alternative Settings

☐ **Home**—Your brother can't find his skateboard and has accused you of taking it without his permission. Using cognitive planning, calmly tell your brother that you didn't take his skateboard. Ask him if he would like you to help him look for it.

☐ **School**—Another student has called you an inappropriate name and stands laughing at you. You feel upset. Remain calm, and think of possible things you could do next. Then, without saying anything, turn and walk away.

☐ **Community**—You are with your family in the mall and have bought soft drinks to carry with you. You accidentally spill yours on a woman's clothing. Give yourself time to think what to say. Then, using a sincere tone of voice, tell her you're sorry you spilled your drink and that you definitely didn't do it on purpose.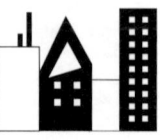

## Skill 1

# Cognitive Planning

**Number of Characters:** 5

**Character Descriptions:**
Ms. Hatch—the classroom teacher
Anthony—a student
Alyssa—a student
Sara—a student
Zeke—a student

**Scene Description:** Two classes have been working together while working on a Civil War project. At the same time, Ms. Hatch's students have been learning about cognitive planning, and they have been practicing using it to work with their classmates from Mr. Gonzalez's classroom. The scene begins after their third class together.

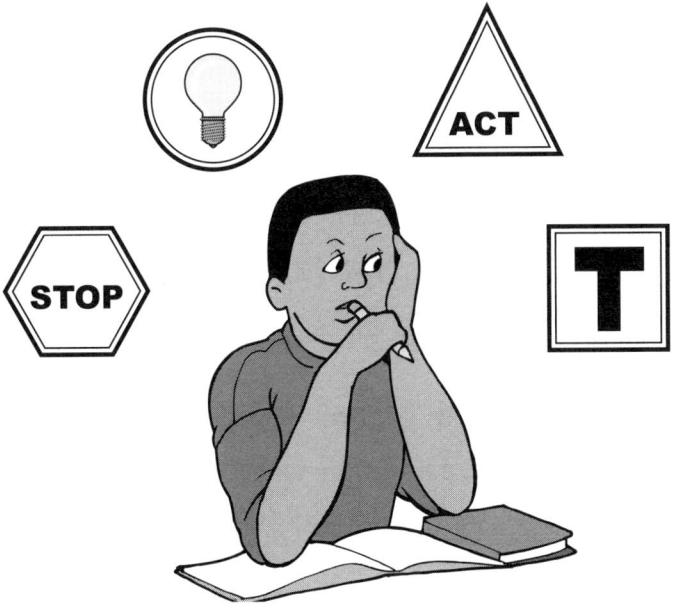

## Skill 1

# Cognitive Planning

MS. HATCH     Let's review the steps you've learned to use when you're working with others. If someone says or does something that makes you angry or hurts your feelings, what are the steps you take in using cognitive planning?

ANTHONY     Think before you act.

MS. HATCH     That's good. That's the second step. Who can tell me the first step?

ALYSSA     Calm down before you do anything else.

MS. HATCH     Yes, that's right. There are two more. Who can tell me what they are?

SARA     One is to act.

MS. HATCH     Can you explain what you mean?

SARA     Tell yourself what would be the best thing to do.

MS. HATCH     Good. What is the last step?

ZEKE     Decide if it worked.

MS. HATCH     Can you tell me what you mean, Zeke?

ZEKE     See how it turned out.

MS. HATCH     Right. Who can tell everyone how you used cognitive planning when we met with Mr. Gonzalez's class?

*Continued on next page*

## Skill 1
# Cognitive Planning—*Continued*

ALYSSA
One of the people in my group said my drawings were stupid. At first, I wanted to tell him he was stupid, too. But I remembered I needed to calm down first.

MS. HATCH
That's great, Alyssa. Then what did you do?

ALYSSA
I counted to 10 and took deep breaths. And then I thought about what I could do next.

MS. HATCH
What did you decide to do?

ALYSSA
I decided to look him in the eye and not say anything.

MS. HATCH
How did it turn out?

ALYSSA
Good! He didn't say anything, and then he looked away. Then Manny told me he thought my drawings were really good, and the rest of the group said they thought so, too.

MS. HATCH
Yes, and your eyes "spoke" for you even though you didn't say anything.

## Skill 2

# Eye Contact

### Definition

Looking at others when you are listening and speaking.

### Activities/Discussions

1. Introduce the concept of appropriate eye contact by asking students to define it. List their ideas on an overhead or on the board. It may be necessary to discuss what *appropriate* means. You may wish to refer to the script for Skill 1.

2. Discuss how different cultural groups use eye contact when speaking and when listening.

3. Have students draw a picture of two people using appropriate eye contact.

------------------------------------------------------------------------------

## Alternative Settings

☐ **Home**—Your grandmother is visiting. She has a picture of your grandfather that she puts on the dresser in the room where she's staying. When you pick it up to look at it, your grandmother starts to cry. Ask her if she wants to tell you why she's crying. Use appropriate eye contact.

☐ **School**—The drawings from your class have been chosen for display during the school art fair. As you are carrying several of them down the hall, you drop them in some water on the floor. Using appropriate eye contact, tell your teacher what happened.

☐ **Community**—You and your family are ordering at a restaurant. Use appropriate eye contact to tell the waitperson what you want to eat.

Scripting Junior © 2004 Thinking Publications
Duplication permitted for educational use only.

## Skill 2

# Eye Contact

**Number of Characters:** 6

**Character Descriptions:** Ms. Sanchez—the classroom teacher
Cody—a student
Melissa—a student
Robert—a student
Will—a student
Narrator

**Props:** Picture of volcano

**Scene Description:** The students in Ms. Sanchez's class have been working on projects about volcanoes. Each student has been assigned to plan a two-minute talk about their project. The scene begins as Ms. Sanchez tells the class what she will be looking for while grading their speeches.

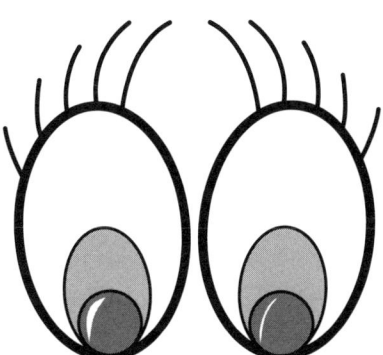

## Skill 2

# Eye Contact

| | |
|---|---|
| MS. SANCHEZ | Today you're going to give your speeches on volcanoes. Remember to use good eye contact. Who can tell me what that means? |
| CODY | It means to look at people. |
| MS. SANCHEZ | When do you look at them? |
| CODY | When you talk to them. |
| MS. SANCHEZ | Yes, do you look at them all the time you're talking? |
| MELISSA | No, first you look at them, and then you look away for a minute. Then you look at them again. |
| MS. SANCHEZ | That's right. Who can tell me what else? |
| ROBERT | You should look at people when you listen. |
| MS. SANCHEZ | Good, let's start. Will, you volunteered to be first. |
| NARRATOR | [Using a picture of a volcano, Will gives his speech to the class. He uses good eye contact.] |
| MS. SANCHEZ | How do you think it went, Will? Did you use appropriate eye contact? |
| WILL | Yeah, I looked at Amy and Cody a couple of times. I looked at you several times. And I looked at Robert. |
| MS. SANCHEZ | I agree, Will. You did a nice job using appropriate eye contact. You looked at several people for just the right amount of time. How did your listeners do? |
| WILL | Some kids were looking down, but most of them looked at me the whole time. |

*Continued on next page*

## Skill 2

# Eye Contact—Continued

Ms. Sanchez   **Did you think people were paying attention to your speech?**

Will   **Mostly.**

Ms. Sanchez   **What do you suggest to your listeners?**

Will   [Looks at his classmates.] **I'd feel better if you'd look at me while I'm giving my speech. When you look away, I'm afraid I've said something wrong, or that you're not interested.**

Ms. Sanchez   **That's good advice, Will. Thank you.**

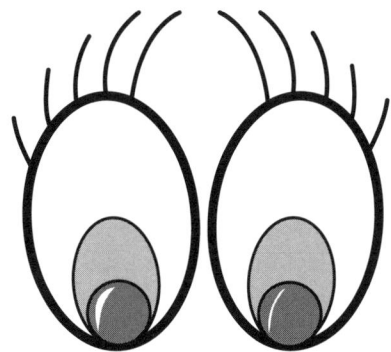

## Skill 3

# Volume

### Definition
Using appropriate voice volumes (quiet, normal, and loud) when speaking in groups.

### Activities/Discussions
1. Introduce the concept of voice volume by asking students to define it.

2. Ask students for examples of how they use voice volume when they speak in varying situations. Discuss situations requiring differing volume levels.

3. Ask three students to volunteer to talk to the class, one using a soft voice; the second using a medium voice; and the third using a loud voice. Discuss which worked the best and why the others didn't work as well.

---

## Alternative Settings

☐ **Home**—Your older sister always shouts when she talks to you. Show how you would tell her that using the correct volume is important. Use the strategies you learned earlier: Calm down, think, act, then evaluate what happened.

☐ **School**—You are going to tell your class about your project on oceans. Show how you will use appropriate voice volume to give your report.

☐ **Community**—You have been trying to find a book in the public library. Using correct voice volume, ask the librarian where it is located.

―― *Skill 3* ――

# Volume

**Number of Characters:** 6

**Character Descriptions:** Mr. Gonzalez—the classroom teacher
Alejandra—a student
Ms. Bell—a guest speaker
Benjamin—a student
Zeke—a student
Narrator

**Scene Description:** Ms. Bell, an expert on whales, is coming to Mr. Gonzalez's class to be interviewed by the students. The scene begins just before Ms. Bell arrives.

## Skill 3

# Volume

| | |
|---|---|
| MR. GONZALEZ | **Alejandra and Benjamin, you'll be interviewing Ms. Bell. Remember to use appropriate voice volume during the interview.** |
| ALEJANDRA AND BENJAMIN | **OK, we will.** |
| NARRATOR | [Ms. Bell arrives.] |
| MR. GONZALEZ | **Hello, Ms. Bell. Thank you for coming to visit us today. Benjamin and Alejandra are going to ask you questions about your work.** |
| ALEJANDRA AND BENJAMIN | [Both use appropriate voice volume.] **Welcome to our class, Ms. Bell.** |
| ALEJANDRA | [Uses appropriate voice volume.] **Ms. Bell, what job do you work at?** |
| MS. BELL | **I study whales: where they live, their migration patterns, and what they eat.** |
| BENJAMIN | [Uses appropriate voice volume.] **What kind of whales do you study?** |
| MS. BELL | **I'm most interested in humpback whales.** |
| BENJAMIN | **Can you tell us where humpback whales live?** |
| MS. BELL | **They live in all the oceans except the polar seas.** |
| ALEJANDRA | **What do humpback whales eat?** |
| MS. BELL | **In Alaska, they eat herring and other small schooling fish, and they eat krill.** |

*Continued on next page* →

## Skill 3

# Volume—Continued

| | |
|---|---|
| ALEJANDRA | What's krill? Is it a fish? |
| MS. BELL | No, krill is the name for very small marine animals. |
| BENJAMIN | How big are the actual fish they eat? |
| MS. BELL | They eat fish up to about 20 centimeters long. Do you know how long that is? |
| ALEJANDRA | No, not really. How big is it? |
| MS. BELL | That's almost 8 inches. |
| ALEJANDRA | Do you have pictures of humpback whales? We were hoping you could show us what they look like. |
| MS. BELL | Yes, I brought these slides to show you. |
| NARRATOR | [Ms. Bell shows her slides to the class and answers questions.] |
| MR. GONZALEZ | Thank you for coming to our class, Ms. Bell. We learned a lot today. |
| NARRATOR | [Ms. Bell leaves.] |
| MR. GONZALEZ | Alejandra, Benjamin, you did a nice job with the interview. How do you think you did with volume? |
| BENJAMIN | Mine seemed to be pretty good. |
| MR. GONZALEZ | I agree. Benjamin, your volume was not too loud and not too soft. Ms. Bell seemed to hear you just fine. Alejandra, how do you think you did? |
| ALEJANDRA | I think mine was OK, too. |
| MR. GONZALEZ | Yes, I think so, too. Ms. Bell seemed to hear you easily, too. |

# Skill 4

# Tone of Voice

## Definition

Using appropriate tone of voice to convey meaning when speaking.

## Activities/Discussions

1. Write these voice tones on an overhead or on the board and ask students to volunteer to demonstrate each:

    - Bossy
    - Excited
    - Firm
    - Sarcastic
    - Whiny

2. Read the following sentences aloud to the students, using the voice tone indicated for each. Ask the students to identify the tone of voice used in each sentence by matching them with the tones you have written:

    - "I can't wait to go to the assembly." (excited)
    - "Can I get a drink?" (whiny)
    - "That's a good idea." (sarcastic)
    - "Put that down." (firm)
    - "You can't do that now." (bossy)

3. Discuss how using different tones of voice can change the meaning of what's being said. Ask students for examples. Have the students use the sentences in #2 to convey different meanings. Review appropriate voice volume from Skill 3.

------------------------------------------------------------------------------

## Alternative Settings

☐ **Home**—Your parents are angry because you forgot to take the trash out in time to be picked up. Use the correct tone of voice to apologize.

☐ **School**—Your teacher has asked you why you handed in an incomplete homework assignment. Use the correct tone of voice to explain why you weren't able to finish it at home.

☐ **Community**—Your mother has asked you to find the flour in the grocery story. Use the correct tone of voice to ask a clerk where to find the flour.

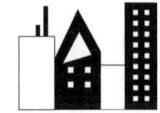

## Skill 4

# Tone of Voice

**Number of Characters:** 4

**Character Descriptions:** Vijay—the pitcher on a softball team
Carla—the catcher on the team
Jason—the first base player on the team
Ms. Williamson—Jason's mother

**Props:** Chairs in the position of van seats; baseball caps for the students

**Scene Description:** Vijay, Carla, and Jason have just finished playing a game their team won. The children are telling Ms. Williamson about the game as she drives them home.

### Tone of Voice Spinner

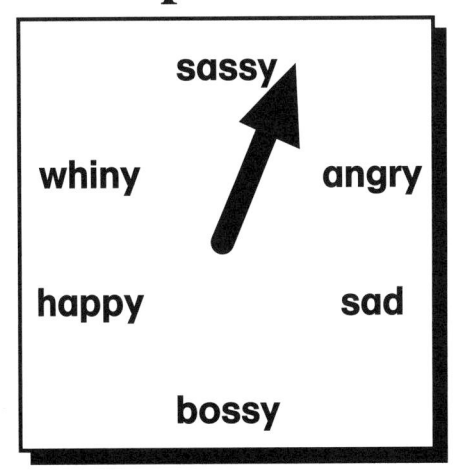

sassy

whiny    angry

happy    sad

bossy

## Skill 4

# Tone of Voice

| | |
|---|---|
| Ms. Williamson | **You guys did great! You all played well today.** |
| Vijay | **[Happily] I'm glad we won!** |
| Carla | **[Excitedly] Me, too! Aren't you glad, Jason?** |
| Jason | **[Happily] Yeah! I'm glad I caught that last out. I was so scared I'd drop it.** |
| Carla | **I know how you feel. [Sadly] I felt bad when I dropped that foul tip. [She's quiet for a few seconds. Then, she says with a lot of feeling.] I couldn't help it, though. I've never caught anything that fast before.** |
| Vijay | **Yeah, I couldn't have caught it, either.** |
| Jason | **Me either. It was really spinning, and that made it even harder to handle.** <br> **[They ride in silence for a few minutes.]** |
| Ms. Williamson | **Did you get any hits?** |
| Jason | **[Excitedly] I got two!** |
| Carla | **I got two, too. [The children giggle about how funny "two, too" sounds.]** |
| Vijay | **I got one, but they caught it. [Happily] At least I didn't strike out.** |
| Ms. Williamson | **Sounds like you had a good game.** |

*Continued on next page*

*Skill 4*

# Tone of Voice—Continued

| | |
|---|---|
| ALL THREE | [Happily] **Yeah!** |
| CARLA | **I can't wait 'til the next game. I'm not going to drop anything.** |
| JASON | **Me, either.** |
| VIJAY | **I hope I get to pitch again. I was pretty good today.** |

## Tone of Voice Spinner

sassy

whiny         angry

happy         sad

bossy

## Skill 5

# Facial Expression

### Definition

Using facial expressions to show how you feel when speaking.

### Activities/Discussions

1. Show your students pictures of different facial expressions, or demonstrate them yourself. Select five or six from the following list:

   - Surprised
   - Sad
   - Tired
   - Confused
   - Afraid
   - Happy
   - Angry
   - Worried
   - Bored
   - Sorry
   - Interested
   - Confident

2. Ask students for examples of facial expressions for the expressions you didn't show or demonstrate.

3. Discuss how using appropriate facial expressions helps us communicate clearly, while using inappropriate facial expressions can lead to problems. Ask for examples. Practice matching volume, tone of voice, and facial expression to reinforce Skills 3 and 4.

---

## Alternative Settings

☐ **Home**—You wanted to see a certain movie, but your sister wanted to see a different one. Your parents ask you to see the movie your sister wants to see. Use an appropriate facial expression to ask them to change their mind. Remember to calm down, think, then act.

☐ **School**—Your teacher has assigned you to a team for your science project. You wanted to be on the same team as your best friend. Use an appropriate facial expression to ask your teacher if you can be switched to your friend's team.

☐ **Community**—You are at a swimming pool and are asked by the lifeguard to get out of the pool for doing something you didn't do. Use an appropriate facial expression to explain that you weren't doing what the lifeguard said you'd done.

# Skill 5

# Facial Expression

**Number of Characters:** 2

**Character Descriptions:** Spencer—a boy
Ms. Newberry—Spencer's mother

**Scene Description:** Spencer's class is going on an overnight camping trip next weekend. He particularly enjoys camping and has been looking forward to the trip. The scene begins when he arrives home from school the day before the trip. NOTE: use the grading terminology practiced in your school.

## Skill 5

# Facial Expression

| | |
|---|---|
| SPENCER | **Hi, Mom.** |
| MS. NEWBERRY | [Happy face] **Hi, Spencer. How was your day?** |
| SPENCER | **Good. I got an A on my math test.** [He grins.] |
| MS. NEWBERRY | **Great! Let me see it. I know you worked hard to learn how to work those problems.** [Proud face] |
| SPENCER | [Shows his mother the test.] **Can we put this on the refrigerator?** |
| MS. NEWBERRY | **Of course. Let's put it up there right now.** [They put the test on the refrigerator.] |
| MS. NEWBERRY | [Hesitates before speaking. Somber face] **Spencer, I'm afraid I have some bad news for you. You're not going to be able to go on the camping trip.** |
| SPENCER | [Disbelieving face] **Why not?** |
| MS. NEWBERRY | **Your dad just called. He's picking us up in 30 minutes to drive us to your grandmother's. She fell and broke her arm, so we're going to go help her for a few days.** |
| SPENCER | [Hopeful face] **But, Mom, couldn't I go camping anyway?** |
| MS. NEWBERRY | [Serious face] **I'm afraid it just won't work, Spencer. We wouldn't be here to pick you up at the bus. And, your dad wants you to help with Grandmom. You know how much she loves seeing you. Your dad thinks seeing you will make her get well faster.** |

**Continued on next page** ➔

## Skill 5

# Facial Expression—Continued

SPENCER [Sad face] **But I'm so disappointed! I've been looking forward to this trip for weeks.**

MS. NEWBERRY **I know you're disappointed. I would be, too.** [Sympathetic] **I'm sorry you can't go.**

SPENCER **Thanks, Mom. I hope I can go on the next one.**

MS. NEWBERRY **I do, too. Maybe you and Dad and I can go camping when we get back from Grandmom's. Would you like that?**

SPENCER [Sad face] **Yeah, that'd be OK. But I wish I could go with my friends.**

MS. NEWBERRY **I know you do. It's not the same, is it? Going with us?**

SPENCER **No.** [His sad face disappears.] **But can I sleep in Grandmother's back yard so I can try out my new sleeping bag?**

MS. NEWBERRY [Laughs.] **I think we can manage that. In fact, let's pack all your camping gear so you can test it out. Then, when you go camping the next time, you'll know what to take.**

## Skill 6

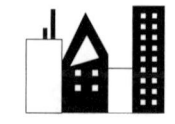

# Posture

### Definition
Using standing and sitting postures that are appropriate for the situation.

### Activities/Discussions

1. Demonstrate confident and unconfident postures for standing and sitting. Ask what you're showing with each posture. Have the class practice these postures, repeating, "Act confident and you'll be confident!"

2. Discuss the meaning of *confidence* and how posture reflects confidence or lack of confidence. Discuss tone of voice, volume, eye contact, and facial expression to reinforce Skills 2–5.

3. Have the students draw a picture of a person using straight posture, and one showing a person using a more relaxed posture.

4. Discuss and demonstrate "angry" posture, "I don't know" posture, and "good listening" posture.

------

## Alternative Settings

☐ **Home**—Your parents have invited some of their friends over for dinner. Use the appropriate posture for sitting at the dinner table and taking part in the conversation.

☐ **School**—Your class has earned a pizza party. Use the appropriate posture for talking to your friends while you eat pizza.

☐ **Community**—You and your father have taken your grandmother to a doctor's appointment. Your father has gone with your grandmother into the examination room. Use the appropriate posture for sitting in the waiting room.

## Skill 6

# Posture

**Number of Characters:** 6

**Character Descriptions:** Mr. Hale—classroom teacher
Anna—a student
Yolanda—a student
Ted—a student
Eric—a student
James—a student

**Scene Description:** Mr. Hale has told the class that they will be demonstrating appropriate postures for different situations. Each student will show the class the appropriate postures for the situations Mr. Hale gives them.

## Skill 6

# Posture

| | |
|---|---|
| MR. HALE | **Anna, are you ready?** |
| ANNA | **Yes.** |
| MR. HALE | **Show me the posture you would use for sitting at the dinner table. You're listening to your sister tell about her day.** [Anna shows a more relaxed sitting posture.] |
| MR. HALE | **How did that feel? Was that appropriate?** |
| ANNA | **Yes. The way I sat showed I'm interested.** |
| MR. HALE | **Does everyone agree? Yolanda?** |
| YOLANDA | **I think she should sit straighter.** |
| MR. HALE | **Why?** |
| YOLANDA | **It shows more interest.** |
| MR. HALE | **What do you think, Anna?** |
| ANNA | **Well, maybe. I guess I could sit straighter.** |
| MR. HALE | **Sitting straight shows more interest. OK, Ted, here's one for you. You are in your classroom, listening to a firefighter talking about fire safety in your home.** [Ted shows a straight sitting posture.] |
| MR. HALE | **Do you think that was appropriate?** |
| TED | **I think so. It showed I'm paying attention.** |

*Continued on next page*

## Skill 6

# Posture—Continued

MR. HALE  **Does everyone agree? Eric?**

ERIC  **Yes, it showed he was interested.**

MR. HALE  **OK, Gretchen, here's one for you. Giving an oral book report to the class.** [Gretchen shows a straight standing posture.]

MR. HALE  **Does that look appropriate? James?**

JAMES  **Yes, it looks right to me.** [All the students show postures for the situations Mr. Hale gives them.]

MR. HALE  **You did a great job. Everyone showed appropriate postures for these situations. The rest of the class showed that they were paying attention by using good eye contact. I'm glad you remembered.**

## Skill 7

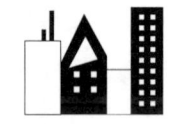

# Personal Space

**Staging**

### Definition
Using distance between people that is appropriate for the situation.

### Activities/Discussions

1. Ask students for examples of the appropriate distance from others to stand in these situations:
   - Telling your friend a secret
   - Talking in front of the class
   - Being introduced to someone you don't know

2. Conduct a discussion of conversational comfort levels, showing how they relate to the distance between the people talking. Reinforce appropriate volume levels.

3. Ask students to describe what they have noticed about the distance people stand from one another when talking or walking.

✂------------------------------------------------------------------

## Alternative Settings

☐ **Home**—Your older brother has brought a new friend of his home for dinner. Show how close to the friend you would stand when you are introduced.

☐ **School**—Your drawing has been selected for an art contest. A local artist is asking each student about their drawing. Show how close you would stand when it is your turn to answer.

☐ **Community**—You are asking a librarian at the public library a question. Show the appropriate distance you would stand while asking the question.

*General Interaction Skills*

Scripting Junior © 2004 Thinking Publications
Duplication permitted for educational use only.

## Skill 7

# Personal Space

**Number of Characters:** 6

**Character Descriptions:** Ms. Jarrett—classroom teacher
Jennifer—a student
Phillip—a student
Keanu—a student
Natalie—a student
Emil—a student

**Scene Description:** Bickler Elementary School is holding an open house for parents and members of the community. A group of Bickler students has been chosen to serve as greeters and guides. At an organizational meeting, the Bickler students are meeting with Ms. Jarrett, a Bickler teacher who has volunteered to help them practice their greeting skills.

## Skill 7

# Personal Space

| | |
|---|---|
| MS. JARRETT | I know you've already learned several of the greeting skills you'll be using. Who can tell me what they are? |
| JENNIFER | Look at the person you're talking to. |
| MS. JARRETT | Do you remember what that's called? |
| JENNIFER | Eye contact. |
| MS. JARRETT | That's right. Who can tell me another greeting skill? |
| PHILLIP | Talk at the right loudness. |
| MS. JARRETT | What is that called? Do you remember? |
| PHILLIP | Yes. It's volume. |
| MS. JARRETT | Yes, it's called volume. Who can tell me another one? |
| KEANU | Facial expression. |
| MS. JARRETT | Yes, facial expression is another greeting skill. You learned about two more. Who can tell me what they are? |
| NATALIE | Posture! |
| MS. JARRETT | Right! Posture is one. What's the last one? |
| EMIL | Personal space? |
| MS. JARRETT | That's right. And who remembers what that means? |
| KEANU | How close you stand when you talk to somebody? |

*Continued on next page*

## Skill 7

# Personal Space—Continued

| | |
|---|---|
| Ms. Jarrett | **Yes. Now let's practice the personal distance you'll use when you greet our visitors.** [She divides the group into pairs.] |
| | **Take turns practicing the greeting. When it's your turn, try standing close, far away, and at arm's length. Then discuss which feels most appropriate.** [Each group practices standing close, at arm's length, and far away as they greet each other.] |
| Ms. Jarrett | **What distance seems best for greeting our visitors?** |
| Natalie | **I felt uncomfortable standing too close, but standing far away doesn't work. I'd say we should stand at arm's length.** |
| Emil | **I agree. We can't shout at them, but we don't want to be too close, either.** |
| Ms. Jarrett | **Does everyone agree? Does at arm's length seem about right for greeting people you don't know?** |
| Jennifer | **It seems right to me.** [Other students agree.] |
| Ms. Jarrett | **OK, everyone practice standing at arm's length— not too close and not too far.** [Students continue practicing.] |

*Skill 8*

# Hygiene

## Definition

Keeping your body and clothes clean.

## Activities/Discussions

1. Post this definition and example of hygiene on an overhead or the board:

    Hygiene—habits leading to healthy living

    Examples: washing hands, bathing, and brushing teeth

2. Ask students for other examples of hygiene and add them to the list. Examples include:

    - Bathing or showering
    - Using dental floss
    - Drinking from your own glass
    - Covering your mouth when you cough
    - Clipping your fingernails
    - Washing your clothes

    - Brushing your teeth
    - Washing your hair
    - Using only your own comb and brush
    - Blowing your nose with a tissue
    - Cleaning your fingernails
    - Flushing the toilet after you use it

3. Conduct a discussion about the importance of hygiene including that it:

    - Reduces the spread of germs
    - Helps us feel better

    - Reduces the chances we'll get sick
    - Helps us look better

## Alternative Settings

☐ **Home**—Your parents have asked you to make a schedule for brushing your teeth. Tell them you'd like to do it two or three times each day.

☐ **School**—Your teacher asks your class to make a hygiene kit to keep in the classroom for student use. List the items you think should be included in the kit.

☐ **Community**—The first day of school is tomorrow. Use your best hygiene to prepare to meet your new teacher and classmates.

― *Skill 8* ―

# Hygiene

**Number of Characters:**  6

**Character Descriptions:**  Dr. Barra—a children's doctor
Tommy—a student
Terese—a student
Zach—a student
Aiden—a student
Daniel—a student

**Props:**  Overhead, poster, dry board, or chalkboard

**Scene Description:**  Dr. Barra, a retired pediatrician, has come to an elementary school class to talk about hygiene. The classroom teacher has already introduced her.

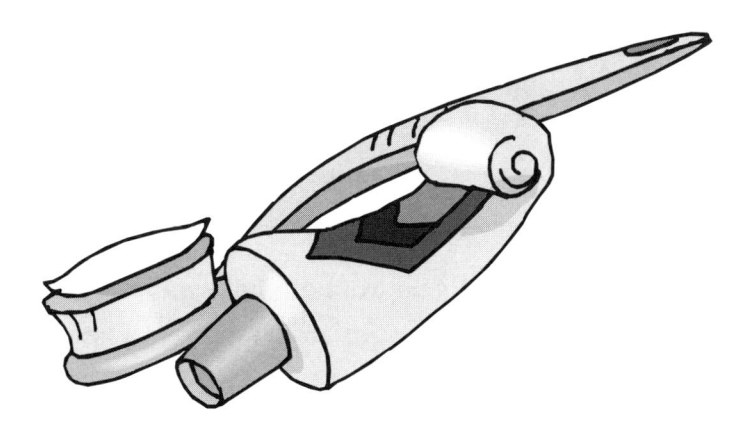

## Skill 8

# Hygiene

| | |
|---|---|
| DR. BARRA | Thank you for inviting me to talk about hygiene. I know you've been studying good personal hygiene. Who can tell me what *hygiene* means? |
| TOMMY | Healthy living? |
| DR. BARRA | That's right. Hygiene means healthy living habits. What are some examples of healthy living habits? |
| TERESE | Wash your hands before you eat. |
| DR. BARRA | Yes, that's a good example. What are some more? |
| ZACH | Use your own glass. |
| DR. BARRA | Right. Those are good examples. I have some more you haven't learned yet.<br>[Dr. Barra writes this list for the class to see: Get a good night's sleep. Eat breakfast. Get plenty of exercise. Eat healthy foods.] |
| DR. BARRA | [Points to "Get a good night's sleep."] What are some ways you can get a good night's sleep? |
| AIDEN | Not staying up too late? |
| DR. BARRA | That's a good example. What's another way you can get a good night's sleep? |
| TERESE | You should make sure it's dark, and it's better if it's quiet in your room. |
| DR. BARRA | Yes, those will both help you get a good night's sleep. [Points to "Eat breakfast."] Who knows what makes a good breakfast? |

*Continued on next page*

## Skill 8

# Hygiene—Continued

| | |
|---|---|
| DANIEL | **I eat cereal and fruit.** |
| DR. BARRA | **Cereal and fruit is good. Can you think of another example?** |
| AIDEN | **What about toast?** |
| DR. BARRA | **Toast by itself might not be enough. If you added some fruit, though, that would be a good breakfast.** |
| DR. BARRA | [Points to "Get plenty of exercise."] **How do you like to get exercise?** |
| TOMMY | **I like to ride my bike.** |
| ZACH | **I ride my bike, too. And I play soccer.** |
| DANIEL | **I play with my cousins all the time. We play tag, and we jump rope a lot.** |
| DR. BARRA | **Those are all good examples.** [Points to "Eat healthy foods".] **Who can tell me some healthy foods?** |
| TOMMY | **The bottom of the food chart we studied showed bread, cereal, rice, and pasta.** |
| DR. BARRA | **Right. What's on the next level?** |
| TERESE | **Fruits and vegetables.** |
| DR. BARRA | **Very good. Are you supposed to eat a lot of chips and candy?** |
| ZACH | **No. Those aren't very healthy, so we're not supposed to eat very many of those.** |
| DR. BARRA | **You seem to know your stuff! If you follow these hygiene rules** [Shows complete list.], **you'll be able to stay healthy, and you'll feel good about yourself.** |

*Skill 9*

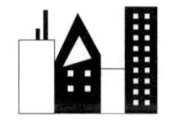

# Body Talk

## Definition
Using different parts of your body to communicate clearly.

## Activities/Discussions

1. Post these aspects of body talk on an overhead or on the board:

   - Eye contact
   - Voice volume
   - Tone of voice
   - Facial expression
   - Posture
   - Personal space
   - Hygiene

2. Review with students what each of these aspects of body talk is and why it's important.

3. Ask students for examples of when they have used each of these aspects of body talk.

---

## Alternative Settings

☐ **Home**—Your favorite cousin is visiting your family. Tell her about the best movie you've seen recently, using your knowledge of body talk to communicate clearly.

☐ **School**—Your teacher has assigned you to give an oral report on a science project you have just completed. Use good body talk to give your report to your classmates.

☐ **Community**—New neighbors with children have just moved in next door. Use appropriate body talk to ask the parents if their children can come over to play with you.

## Skill 9

# Body Talk

**Number of Characters:** 3

**Character Descriptions:** Dad—parent of Seth and Amber
Seth—a boy
Amber—a girl

**Scene Description:** The scene takes place at home. The family has been invited to a barbecue at the home of the mother's boss, Mr. Harris. The father is helping his son and daughter get ready for the barbecue.

## Skill 9

# Body Talk

| | |
|---|---|
| DAD | Are you almost ready? We have to leave in five minutes. |
| SETH | I'm ready! |
| DAD | Did you put on clean clothes after you took a shower? |
| SETH | Yeah. |
| DAD | And did you wash your hair in the shower? |
| SETH | Yes, and I cleaned under my fingernails, too. |
| DAD | Great job, Seth! Amber, you look neat and clean. How are you going to stand when you're introduced to Mr. Harris? |
| AMBER | Not too close and not too far. |
| DAD | Right. Anything else? |
| AMBER | I'll stand up straight, too. |
| DAD | Yes. Good job. Seth, what are you going to do with your eyes? |
| SETH | I'm going to look at him when he talks. |
| DAD | Yes! And how will you use your voice? |
| SETH | I won't yell. |
| DAD | [Smiles.] That's good news. One more thing. What about your faces? |
| AMBER | We should look happy to meet him. |
| DAD | How will that look? |

[Seth and Amber show him happy faces.]

*Continued on next page*

## Skill 9

# Body Talk—*Continued*

DAD  **OK, let's role-play. Seth, you pretend I'm Mr. Harris. Amber, you introduce us.**

AMBER  [Looks at Seth's Dad.] **Mr. Harris, this is Seth.** [Turns to Seth.] **Seth, this is Mr. Harris.**

SETH  [Looks at Dad with a pleasant expression on his face. Uses an appropriate volume and tone of voice.] **How do you do, Mr. Harris. I'm pleased to meet you.**

DAD  [Pretending to be Mr. Harris] **Hello, Seth. It's nice to meet you, too.**

DAD  **Nice, job, Seth.** [Turns to Amber.] **Amber, do you want to try it out, too?**

AMBER  **I think I know what to do. It helped to watch you, Seth.**

DAD  **OK, I think we're ready to go. Let's get Mom.**

## Skill 10

# Manners

### Definition
Behaving in a polite and respectful way when interacting with others.

### Activities/Discussions

1. List these examples of manners on an overhead or on the board:

   - Saying, "Please"
   - Saying, "Excuse me"
   - Using a napkin on your lap
   - Not slurping with a straw
   - Keeping elbows off the table
   - Saying, "Thank you"
   - Saying, "I'm sorry"
   - Chewing with your mouth closed
   - Talking at the appropriate volume

2. Discuss what these examples have in common; conclude with the concept of manners. Discuss why manners are important, including the idea of showing respect to others.

3. Ask students for examples of manners they would use when they're in a restaurant.

4. Discuss the use of facial expression, posture, tone of voice, and voice volume in practicing good manners.

------

## Alternative Settings

☐ **Home**—Your sister is trying to make a good impression on her new friend. The three of you are deciding what TV show to watch. Use appropriate manners when you tell them which program you want to watch.

☐ **School**—Your principal has come to your class to hear about an idea to begin a schoolwide recycling program. Use good manners as you tell her your ideas for the program and ask for her help in getting it started.

☐ **Community**—You are sitting between two older people at a church dinner. Use good manners when you ask them to pass you different dishes of food.

## Skill 10

# Manners

**Number of Characters:** 4

**Character Descriptions:** Aunt Tony—the children's great aunt
Uncle Denzel—the children's great uncle
Amir—a seven-year-old boy
Lakeisha—a nine-year-old girl

**Scene Description:** A family reunion. The children have never met their great-aunt and great-uncle before.

*Please*
*Thank You*
*Excuse Me*

# Skill 10

# Manners

| | |
|---|---|
| AUNT TONY | You must be Amir! I'm Aunt Tony, and this is Uncle Denzel. |
| AMIR | Yes, hello. |
| AUNT TONY | And you're Lakeisha, I bet. It's nice to meet you. |
| LAKEISHA | Yes, ma'am. |
| UNCLE DENZEL | Hello, Amir. [They shake hands.] What grade are you in? |
| AMIR | [Stands up straight. Looks at Uncle Denzel.] I'm in fourth grade. |
| UNCLE DENZEL | [Shakes hands with Lakeisha.] What about you, Lakeisha? What grade are you in? |
| LAKEISHA | I'm in third grade this year. |
| AUNT TONY | What are you studying this year, Lakeisha? |
| LAKEISHA | [Continues standing straight. Looks at Aunt Tony.] We've been studying the oceans, mostly weather patterns, animal life, habitats, and endangered species. Next we're going to track a hurricane. |
| AUNT TONY | Track a hurricane! How will you do that? |
| LAKEISHA | We'll keep track of the time, coordinates, and wind speed so we can predict when it will hit land. |
| AUNT TONY | That's pretty impressive. [Turns to Amir.] What about you, Amir? What are you studying? |
| AMIR | [Excitedly] We're studying ancient civilizations, and we're making our own Stonehenge calendar! |
| AUNT TONY | Wow, that's interesting! How are you doing it? |

*Continued on next page*

## Skill 10

# Manners—Continued

| | |
|---|---|
| AMIR | [Looks back and forth between Aunt Tony and Uncle Denzel. Stands straight.] **First we made a center point and used a compass to put rocks at each direction around the middle point. Next week we get to put in the sunset markers so we can start the calendar at the winter solstice.** |
| AUNT TONY | **That's a lot more interesting than when I was in school. What class is this for?** |
| AMIR | **It's for my science class.** |
| UNCLE DENZEL | **You both sound like you're good students.** |
| LAKEISHA AND AMIR | **Thank you!** |
| AUNT TONY | **Well, we'd better find your mom. I haven't seen her yet. Do you know where she is?** |
| LAKEISHA | **She's talking to Grandpa Washington. Would you like us to show you where they are?** |
| AUNT TONY | **Please. I'd appreciate that. Amir, are you coming?** |
| AMIR | **Yes, ma'am.** |
| AUNT TONY | **Denzel, what are you going to do?** |
| UNCLE DENZEL | **I think I'll come along with you,** [Looks at Lakeisha.] **if you don't mind.** |
| LAKEISHA | **Yes, sir, that would be just fine.** |
| AUNT TONY | [Walking behind Lakeisha and Amir, whispers to Uncle Denzel.] **Aren't they polite children?** |
| UNCLE DENZEL | [Whispers to Aunt Tony.] **They sure are. I like them already, don't you?** |
| AUNT TONY | [Whispers to Uncle Denzel.] **Oh, yes, they're such nice kids.** |

*Skill 11*

# Listening Basics

### Definition
Hearing and thinking about what someone is saying.

### Activities/Discussions
1. Ask students to define *listening*, eliciting responses characteristic of the cultural groups represented in the class. List their responses on an overhead or on the board. Review eye contact, body talk, posture, and facial expression.

2. Ask students to draw a self-portrait showing how they look when they listen well.

3. Discuss how it feels when someone doesn't seem to be listening to us.

------

## Alternative Settings

☐ **Home**—Your best friend is telling you how sad she/he feels because her/his favorite grandmother has died. Show how you will let her/him know you are listening to what she/he is saying. Remember to calm down, think, and then act.

☐ **School**—Your classmates are giving oral book reports. Show how you will sit and what you will do with your body to show you are listening.

☐ **Community**—You have gone with your best friend to her cousin's house for dinner. Show how you will let her cousin's family know you are listening as they talk during dinner.

## Skill 11

# Listening Basics

**Number of Characters:** 9

**Character Descriptions:** Mr. Jones—story reader
Aunt Lily—the children's aunt
Carlos—a boy
Vanessa—a girl
Two boys and two girls at the story time
Narrator

**Props:** Picture of a cat; picture of a dog; a book

**Scene Description:** Two children have gone with their aunt to a children's story time at the public library. Several other children are in the audience.

## Skill 11

# Listening Basics

| | |
|---|---|
| MR. JONES | **Hello, boys and girls!** |
| ALL THE CHILDREN | **Hello!** |
| MR. JONES | **I'm going to read you a story about a dog whose friend, the cat, is lost. Here is the dog.** [Points to a picture of the dog.] **And here is the cat.** [Points to a picture of the cat]. **The dog is worried, so he goes to find his friend.** [Continues to show pictures throughout the story.] |
| NARRATOR | [Carlos sits facing Mr. Jones. He looks at Mr. Jones's face and the book Mr. Jones is holding. Vanessa lies down on the floor.] |
| AUNT LILY | **Vanessa, can you show Mr. Jones how you can listen?** |
| NARRATOR | [Vanessa sits up and looks at Mr. Jones.] |
| AUNT LILY | **That's great!** |
| VANESSA | **Do you know the dog's name?** |
| NARRATOR | [All the children shake their heads, "No."] |
| MR. JONES | **His name is Travis of Travis Heights. And his friend's name is Lucy.** |
| NARRATOR | [Carlos looks at Mr. Jones as he raises his hand.] |
| MR. JONES | **Thank you for raising your hand. That's good manners. Do you have a question?** |
| CARLOS | [Looks at Mr. Jones as he talks.] **Yes. I thought dogs chased cats!** |
| MR. JONES | **Hmmm. This dog is different, isn't he? Let's see what happens in the story.** |
| NARRATOR | [Mr. Jones reads the story about Travis and Lucy. Travis goes to several places and looks for Lucy. Using good manners, he asks a dragon if he's seen her. He asks a gecko if she's seen her. He asks several others if they've seen her. Everyone says, "No." Finally, Travis sees Lucy's tail and catches up with her. They go back home.] |

*Continued on next page* ➔

## Skill 11

# Listening Basics—*Continued*

NARRATOR [The children sit up straight and look at Mr. Jones telling the story. They look at the book to see the pictures. Then they look at Mr. Jones again. They do this until Mr. Jones is finished.]

MR. JONES **What do you think about this story?**

NARRATOR [Carlos thinks about the question for a few seconds, then puts his hand up.]

MR. JONES [To Carlos] **Yes? What do you think?**

CARLOS **I liked the story because it's different from other stories.**

MR. JONES **Can you explain what you mean?**

CARLOS [Thinks a few seconds before answering.] **I've never seen pictures like these before, and the dog keeps asking people if they've seen the cat. It's like he's on an adventure.**

NARRATOR [Vanessa raises her hand and waits to be called on.]

MR. JONES [To Vanessa] **What would you like to say?**

VANESSA **I liked the cat because she wasn't really lost at all. She was trying to find some fish.**

MR. JONES **Do you think there might be two adventures happening in this story?**

CARLOS [Thinks about the question.] **Yes, I can see what you mean.**

VANESSA [Also thinks about the question before answering.] **Yes, both the dog and the cat have an adventure.**

MR. JONES **You certainly listened well, and I enjoyed reading the story to you. You watched my face and looked at the book, you raised your hands with questions, and you used appropriate facial expressions. You were a terrific audience!**

## Skill 12

# Staying On and Switching Topics

### Definition
Talking about the same idea or topic. Talking about a new idea or topic.

### Activities/Discussions

1. Brainstorm with students to compile a list of ideas or topics they like to talk about.

2. Choose one of the topics from the list, and write it in a circle in the middle of an overhead or on the board. Draw four lines coming out from the circle. Ask students four details they could say about it, writing one on each of the lines. Repeat this exercise for another topic.

3. Discuss how each of the four details is related to its topic. Then ask students to describe how they would change from talking about one topic to talking about one of the others listed. Discuss how staying on topic is good manners and lets people know you are a good listener.

---

## Alternative Settings

☐ **Home**—Your older brother has asked you what you think about the music he's listening to on the radio. Tell him four things you like about the music, making sure all your comments deal with the topic.

☐ **School**—Your teacher has asked you to describe to the class your favorite character in a book. Tell your classmates four things about a character. Make sure everything you say is related to the character.

☐ **Community**—You have been selected to guide a tour of parents visiting your school. Prepare a list of the things you would tell them about the school, grouping them into topics (e.g., history, architecture, special programs, graduates).

## Skill 12

# Staying On and Switching Topics

**Number of Characters:** 5

**Character Descriptions:** Ruben—a student at Monroe Elementary School
Dong—a student at Monroe Elementary School
Isabel—a student at Monroe Elementary School
Mr. Salas—a resident of the center
Mrs. Jacobs—a resident of the center

**Props:** 2 chairs (for Mr. Salas and Mrs. Jacobs); a TV

**Scene Description:** A class is making its first visit to a nearby assisted-living center. Two of the residents have asked the children about themselves.

## Skill 12

# Staying On and Switching Topics

| | |
|---|---|
| MRS. JACOBS | Hello, who are you? |
| DONG | Hello. My name is Dong. This is Ruben, and this is Isabel. |
| MR. SALAS | Are you from Monroe Elementary? |
| RUBEN | Yes. Mrs. Pugh is our teacher. |
| MR. SALAS | What subjects are you studying in school? |
| DONG | We have reading, and math, and spelling, and science. We have PE on Monday, Wednesday, and Friday. And Ms. Zheng teaches us art on Tuesday and Thursday. We get to go to drama and music every other week. |
| MRS. JACOBS | That sounds like a lot of subjects. |
| ISABEL | [Looks at Mrs. Jacobs.] I like math the best. It's easy. |
| RUBEN | Not for me! I like spelling better. |
| DONG | [Uses appropriate volume.] My favorite is art. But I like music, too. |
| MR. SALAS | How did you get here from your school? Did you walk over, or did you ride the bus? |
| RUBEN | We walked with our teacher. We had to stay together. |
| MRS. JACOBS | Was it cold? |
| DONG | [Uses good posture.] It's not too cold. Mrs. Pugh told us to wear our jackets, but I was too hot. Last week, we walked to the park for science class. It was really cold then. |
| ISABEL | I didn't want to go outside. |
| RUBEN | I didn't either. Ms. Fry made us run fast! |
| MR. SALAS | Did you keep warm? |
| RUBEN | Yes, I was so warm I unzipped my jacket. |
| ISABEL | Not me. I kept my hood on! I was cold! |

*Continued on next page*

# Skill 12

# Staying On & Switching Topics—*Continued*

| | |
|---|---|
| DONG | [Looks at the television that Mr. Salas and Mrs. Jacobs had been watching.] **What are you watching?** |
| MRS. JACOBS | **Oh, just a soap opera. We don't need to see it right now, do we Mr. Salas?** |
| MR. SALAS | **No. I'd rather talk to you children.** |
| ISABEL | **May I ask you a question? Why is it called a "soap opera"?** |
| MRS. JACOBS | [Laughs.] **Oh, these shows used to be sponsored by soap companies, and they're just like operas because they're sentimental, I guess. What do you think, Mr. Salas?** |
| MR. SALAS | **I'm not sure these children know what "sentimental" means. Should I tell you?**<br>[All three children nod.] |
| MR. SALAS | **It means using your feelings instead of your head to guide your actions. So people acting from sentiment don't always think before they act.** |
| MRS. JACOBS | **Have you ever seen your mother cry when you do something nice for her? That's an example of being sentimental. She's crying because she's happy. She doesn't stop to think how she should act. It just comes naturally.** |
| DONG | **So, are operas sentimental, too?** |
| MRS. JACOBS | **Some of them are, but some of them are funny.** |
| ISABEL | **Is it wrong to be sentimental?** |
| MRS. JACOBS | **Not really. I am sometimes.** |
| RUBEN | **This is changing the subject, but do you get to watch movies?** |
| MR. SALAS | **Sure, we watch a movie almost every night after dinner, don't we Mrs. Jacobs?** |
| MRS. JACOBS | **Yes. Tonight we're watching *Gone with the Wind* again. We've seen it many times, but it's always good.** |
| ISABEL | **What's it about?** [They continue their conversation until their teacher tells them it's time to leave.] |

*Skill 13*

# Conversations

### Definition
Starting conversations with a greeting. Taking turns talking and listening. Ending with a farewell.

### Activities/Discussions

1. Brainstorm different ways of greeting others, guiding them to focus on formal and informal greetings. Group ideas into formal and informal on an overhead or the board. Discuss settings where each type of greeting is appropriate. Review the previous skills and how they are used in formal and informal greetings. Repeat with examples of farewells.

2. Have students select a greeting and a farewell from both the formal and the informal list. Group them into pairs. Assign each student either the formal or the informal role. Tell them each will have a turn, using the following format:

   - Formal uses a formal greeting, says three things about a book or comic book they've just read, and uses a formal farewell.

   - Informal uses an informal greeting, says three things about a movie they've just seen, and uses an informal farewell.

3. Discuss the need for taking turns talking and listening in a conversation.

---

## Alternative Settings

☐ **Home**—Your mother is working on the family checkbook. Show how you would ask her if you can go to your friend's house to play. Use a greeting, ask her if you can go, and use a farewell when the conversation is over.

☐ **School**—A guest is observing your classroom. Your teacher selects you to escort him to a classroom on the other side of the building. Show how you would talk to him. Begin with a greeting, and use a farewell when you leave him at the other classroom.

☐ **Community**—You are at the grocery store with your dad. You see your school principal coming toward you. Introduce her to your dad using a greeting, the introduction, and a farewell when you are finished.

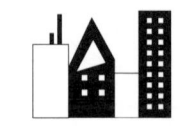

## Skill 13

# Conversations

**Number of Characters:** 6

**Character Descriptions:** Ms. Perez—a classroom teacher
Mr. Williams—a classroom teacher
Erik—a student
Emily—a student
Nicholas—a student
Sam—a student

**Scene Description:** Ms. Perez has taken her class to Mr. Williams's classroom. The two teachers are co-teaching a unit on conversations. The scene begins when the two classes meet each other for the first time. The teachers have paired each student from Ms. Perez's class with one from Mr. Williams's class.

## Skill 13

# Conversations

| | |
|---|---|
| MR. WILLIAMS | Welcome, Ms. Perez. Welcome, students. |
| MS. PEREZ | Let's begin by getting to know each other. Students from both classes have been working on conversations. Who remembers what to include in a conversation? |
| ERIK | You start a conversation with a greeting. |
| MR. WILLIAMS | Right. You start with a greeting. Then what? |
| EMILY | You take turns talking and listening. |
| MR. WILLIAMS | Yes, you take turns talking and listening. Who knows how to end a conversation? |
| NICHOLAS | With an ending. |
| MS. PEREZ | What's the ending called, Nicholas? |
| NICHOLAS | A farewell? |
| MS. PEREZ | Right, you end with a farewell. Let's practice. Begin with a greeting. Be sure to include your partner's name. Then you take turns talking and listening. At the end of the conversation, use a farewell. |
| SAM | But we're not leaving! How can we use a farewell? |
| MR. WILLIAMS | You're right, Sam. We're not leaving yet. We're just practicing conversations right now. This will help you learn how to include everything in a conversation. OK, go ahead. Remember to use all three parts of a conversation. [The students practice using a greeting, taking turns talking and listening, and using a farewell. Ms. Perez tells them to stop.] |
| MS. PEREZ | Let's hear what you did. What greetings did you use? |
| EMILY | Sam said, "Hi, Emily, my name is Sam. It's nice to meet you." |
| MR. WILLIAMS | Oh, Sam used a formal greeting. How did that make you feel? |

*Continued on next page*

# Skill 13

# Conversations—Continued

| | |
|---|---|
| EMILY | Good! I felt special. |
| MR. WILLIAMS | I'll bet. What's another greeting you used? |
| ERIK | Nicholas said, "Hi, Erik, how's it going?" |
| MS. PEREZ | That was more informal than Sam's greeting. How did that make you feel? |
| ERIK | I liked it. I felt like we'd be friends. |
| MS. PEREZ | That sounds good. Then what did you say? |
| SAM | I said, "What's your favorite class in school?" |
| MR. WILLIAMS | Good. Did you practice taking turns talking? |
| NICHOLAS | We did. I said, "I really like that drawing. Did you do it?" And Erik said, "Yes, do you like to draw?" Then we talked about drawing awhile. |
| EMILY | I asked Sam what his best subject is, and he told me it was math. |
| MS. PEREZ | Those are good examples of taking turns. Did anyone use a formal farewell? |
| ERIK | We did. We practiced saying, "Goodbye. I'm glad we had a chance to talk." And, "Goodbye. I'm happy to have met you." |
| MR. WILLIAMS | How did that feel? |
| NICHOLAS | It felt kind of funny at first, but I'm glad we practiced saying it. I feel like I have a better idea how to end a conversation with somebody I've just met. |
| MS. PEREZ | I'm glad you tried it out. Next time we practice, you'll feel even more confident. Don't you agree, Mr. Williams? |
| MR. WILLIAMS | I certainly do. You're getting better each day. You used the right volume, you watched each other's faces, and you were the right distance apart. |

## Skill 14

# Interrupting

### Definition
Politely breaking in on someone's conversations or actions.

### Activities/Discussions

1. Ask students what they think *interrupt* means. Have them draw a picture of one person interrupting a conversation between other people.

2. Ask students for examples of when it's OK to interrupt, and list them on an overhead or on the board under OK. Ask them for examples of when it's not OK to interrupt, and list them under Not OK.

3. For each of the examples under OK, ask students how they would politely interrupt. Reinforce voice volume, tone of voice, personal space, and manners in the discussion.

------

## Alternative Settings

☐ **Home**—Your mom is outside talking to the next-door neighbor. Politely interrupt her to tell her your dad is on the phone and wants to talk to her.

☐ **School**—Two teachers are talking together on the playground. Politely interrupt them to tell them you've skinned your knee and need to see the nurse or health aide.

☐ **Community**—A clerk is stocking shelves in the grocery store. Politely interrupt her to ask where the toothpaste is located.

# Skill 14

# Interrupting

**Number of Characters:** 3

**Character Descriptions:** Rebecca—a girl
Mr. Green—Rebecca's father
Mr. Sandoval—Mr. Green's boss

**Scene Description:** Rebecca has gone with her father to National Take-Your-Child-to-Work Day. Her father works in the printing division at the local newspaper. The father is talking to his boss, Mr. Sandoval. Rebecca needs to interrupt to ask where the restroom is. Emphasize the appropriate use of body language, posture, tone of voice, and voice volume.

## Skill 14

# Interrupting

| | |
|---|---|
| MR. GREEN | The paper order just came in, Frank. Where do you want the paperwork? |
| MR. SANDOVAL | I'll take it now. Has that ink order gotten here yet? |
| MR. GREEN | Not yet. They said it should be here today. |
| MR. SANDOVAL | Let me know when it gets here. We need it by 2:00. I want you to stay here, though, George. There's a group of students coming through in about 15 minutes, and I want you to show them how the presses work. |
| REBECCA | Excuse me, Dad, Mr. Green. I'm sorry to interrupt. Where is the restroom? |
| MR. GREEN | It's just around that corner, honey. [Points.] See? |
| REBECCA | Yes. Thanks, Dad. |
| MR. GREEN | I'll be right here when you get back. |
| | [Rebecca goes to the restroom.] |
| MR. SANDOVAL | She's sure polite. It's nice to see such a polite child. |
| MR. GREEN | Thank you. We're really proud of her. |
| MR. SANDOVAL | Is she your oldest? |
| MR. GREEN | No, Phil is two years older. |
| MR. SANDOVAL | Why didn't you bring him today? |

*Continued on next page*

## Skill 14

# Interrupting—Continued

MR. GREEN      He's with his mom. He wanted to see where she works.

MR. SANDOVAL   Well, Rebecca is certainly polite. Tell her I said goodbye.

MR. GREEN      OK, I will. See you later, Frank.
               [Rebecca returns.]

MR. GREEN      Mr. Sandoval said to tell you goodbye. He also said how polite you were. You used just the right voice and body language.

# Skill 15

# Right Time and Place

## Definition
Doing and saying things that are appropriate for the situation you're in.

## Activities/Discussions

1. Discuss situations exhibiting appropriate and inappropriate behavior. List these on an overhead or on the board:

   - Run around and act silly
   - Talk loudly
   - Comb hair
   - Sit quietly and listen
   - Tell a joke
   - Make slurping noises
   - Bounce a ball
   - Whisper

   Discuss why it is important to calm down and think about when and where these actions are appropriate.

2. Ask students to describe (list on an overhead or the board) the appropriate time and place to:

   - Tell their teacher they lost their homework assignment
   - Tell their parents they got all *A*s on their report card
   - Ask their older brother to take them for ice cream
   - Ask a friend for help with spelling

   Discuss what could happen if they didn't think before they acted.

---

## Alternative Settings

☐ **Home**—You want your best friend to come over to spend the night. Describe the appropriate time and place to ask your parents. Then show how you would talk to them.

☐ **School**—You want your teacher to help you choose an idea for a math project. Describe an appropriate time and place to talk to her. Then show how you would talk to her. Discuss whether it would be good to interrupt her for this reason.

☐ **Community**—You lost one of your sandals at the swimming pool and have gone to ask the pool assistant if he's seen it. Describe an appropriate time and place to talk to him. Then show how you would talk to him.

— Skill 15 —

# Right Time and Place

**Setting**

**Number of Characters:** 8

**Character Descriptions:** Patel—a student
Ms. Ruiz—a guide at the zoo
Sarah—a student
Jared—a student
Samantha—a student
Eden—a student
Caroline—a student
Mr. Carlson—a teacher

**Props:** Tape measure or meter stick

**Scene Description:** A class has just finished a guided tour of the zoo. The guide, Ms. Ruiz, is showing a red-tailed hawk's nest to the class and to Mr. Carlson, their teacher. Several students are talking to Ms. Ruiz about the nest. Caroline joins the group in the middle of the conversation.

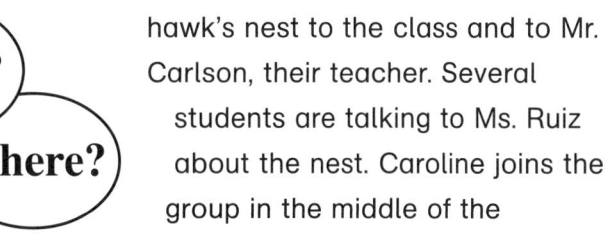

*General Interaction Skills*

## Skill 15

# Right Time and Place

| | |
|---|---|
| PATEL | [Looking at the nest] **It's so big!** |
| MS. RUIZ | **How far across do you think it is?** |
| SARAH | **Two feet?** |
| MS. RUIZ | **Bigger than that. The male and female can each be almost two feet long. They need a nest that is big enough for them and the baby hawks.** |
| JARED | **This looks huge!** |
| MS. RUIZ | **Let's measure it.** [They use a tape measure to measure across the nest.] **What does it say?** |
| SAMANTHA | **Wow! It's almost 38 inches across!** |
| MS. RUIZ | **They're big birds, alright. What materials do you see in the nest?** |
| JARED | **I see some cloth. And a bright thing; I can't tell what it is.** |
| MS. RUIZ | **Um hmm. What else?** |
| EDEN | **Lots of feathers.** |
| MS. RUIZ | **Yes. There are a lot of feathers. Anything else?** |
| SARAH | **I see some twigs, too.** [Caroline walks up to the group.] |
| MS. RUIZ | **That's right. These hawks use a lot of different materials to make their nests, including fresh bark and pine needles.** |
| CAROLINE | **Excuse me, Ms. Ruiz. May I ask you a question?** |

*Continued on next page*

## Skill 15

# Right Time and Place—*Continued*

MS. RUIZ     **Sure. What is it?**

CAROLINE     **What color are the babies when they hatch?**

MS. RUIZ     **They're usually gray and white with black beaks and dark eyes.**

CAROLINE     **When do their tails turn red?**

MS. RUIZ     **They're about two years old before that happens. Their tails are brown and white until then.**

CAROLINE     **Thank you.**

MS. RUIZ     **You're welcome. Any more questions?**

CAROLINE     **May I look at the nest up close?**

MS. RUIZ     **Sure, if it's OK with your teacher.** [Ms. Ruiz looks at Mr. Carlson. He nods his head yes. Caroline joins the other students gathered around the nest.]

## Skill 16

# Being Formal or Casual

### Definition
Knowing when to be more proper and respectful (formal); or more relaxed and casual (informal).

### Activities/Discussions
1. Write on an overhead or the board: *formal* and *casual*. Brainstorm with students examples of proper and respectful language, and write them under *formal*. Then brainstorm examples of natural, relaxed, and casual language, and write them under *casual*. Discuss clues used to decide whether a situation calls for formal or informal language. Examples include:

   - Clothes people are wearing
   - Relationships among the people (e.g., degree of familiarity; power and authority)
   - Setting (e.g., church, sporting event, party, restaurant)
   - Nature of the event (e.g., funeral, wedding, birthday party, grocery story)

2. Discuss what communication skills are best in formal and informal settings (e.g., posture, volume, etc.)

---

## Alternative Settings

☐ **Home**—*Formal:* Your parents are having a special anniversary party for your grandparents. They've asked you to greet people when they arrive. Use formal language to greet the guests.

*Casual:* Your parents have said you can invite your friend over for dinner. Call your friend on the phone and use informal language to invite her or him.

☐ **School**—*Formal:* Your class has invited a guest speaker. You have been assigned to greet the guest. Use formal language to introduce yourself.

*Casual:* You are walking home with your friend. Use informal language to talk about a book you're reading.

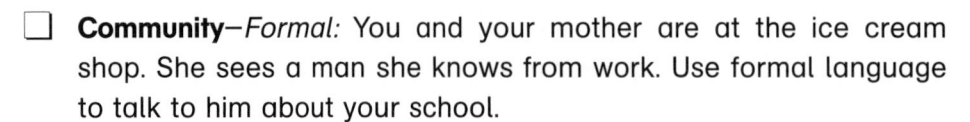

☐ **Community**—*Formal:* You and your mother are at the ice cream shop. She sees a man she knows from work. Use formal language to talk to him about your school.

*Casual:* You and your older sister are at the video store. you see one of your friends from school. Use informal language to tell your friend about the movie you and your sister are renting.

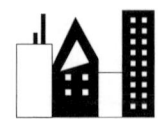

## Skill 16

# Being Formal or Casual

**Number of Characters:** 7

**Character Descriptions:** Duval—a boy
Charles—a boy
Man—spectator at the fireworks
Mr. Simmons—Charles's father
Ms. Simmons—Charles's mother
Amanda—Charles's younger sister
Andrea—a friend of Amanda

**Props:** Blankets; basket; cooler or tote bag

**Scene Description:** Duval has gone to watch the fireworks with his friend Charles and Charles's family. There are only a few spots left on the grass for them to put their blankets. The parents ask the two older children to put their blankets down while they carry the food from the car.

## Skill 16

# Being Formal or Casual

| | |
|---|---|
| DUVAL | **It's pretty crowded. Looks like we'll have to squeeze in there.** [Points to a spot between two other groups.] |
| CHARLES | **Do you think they'll mind?** [Looks at the people around the spot.] |
| DUVAL | **Let's ask them. We don't know them very well. Hey, let's practice using formal language like we learned in school.** [They walk to the open spot.] |
| DUVAL | **Excuse me. Would you mind if we put our blankets here?** |
| MAN | **Not at all. We'll scoot over.** |
| CHARLES | **Thank you.** [Their parents and younger sisters arrive.] |
| MR. SIMMONS | [To the man next to them] **Thank you for moving over. We really appreciate it.** |
| MAN | **You're welcome. There's plenty of room.** |
| MS. SIMMONS | **Thanks so much!** [Turns to Duval and Charles.] **You boys must have made a good impression. How'd you do it?** |
| CHARLES | **Duval used the formal language we're learning in class.** |
| MS. SIMMONS | **Nice job, boys! I guess you can relax now, though.** [Duval and Charles both nod.] |
| CHARLES | **Hey, Amanda, what've you got?** |
| AMANDA | **The lemonade.** |
| DUVAL | **Go, girl! That looks heavy!** |
| ANDREA | **I've got the napkins!** |
| CHARLES | **Good for you. We'll need them!** |

*Continued on next page*

## Skill 16

# Being Formal or Casual—Continued

| | |
|---|---|
| Ms. Simmons | **Hey, boys, I found the Frisbee™.** |
| Duval | **Oh, thanks, Ms. Simmons. Can we go play for awhile?** |
| Ms. Simmons | **Sure. I'll come with you.** |
| Charles | **Yeah! Let's go, guys!** |
| Mr. Simmons | **I'll whistle when we're ready to eat, OK?** |
| Ms. Simmons | **Sounds good. We won't be far.** |
| | [Ms. Simmons and the boys go off to play with the Frisbee. Mr. Simmons and the girls begin unpacking the picnic.] |
| Mr. Simmons | [Whistles to Ms. Simmons that the picnic is ready.] |
| Ms. Simmons | **OK, boys, time to go eat!** |
| Charles and Duval | **Yea!** |

*Skill 17*

# Optimism

## Definition

Choosing to have mostly positive thoughts.

## Activities/Discussions

1. Ask students what they think *self-talk* means. Lead them to understand that self-talk is how we explain things to ourselves.

2. Ask students for examples of positive and negative self-talk. Have them draw a picture of how their face looks when they use positive self-talk and one showing how they look when they use negative self-talk.

3. Write on an overhead or on the board: *optimism* and *pessimism*. Ask students which type of talk (positive or negative) they think goes with each word. Discuss how positive self-talk is related to optimism and negative self-talk is related to pessimism. Discuss the importance of optimism.

## Alternative Settings

☐ **Home**—Your parents told you that you could go play with your friend after school today. When you get home from school, your dad tells you that you can't go. Describe how you can show optimism about the situation. Don't forget good manners and body language.

☐ **School**—You have trouble understanding a science lesson and stay after class to ask your science teacher for help. Show an optimistic attitude when you talk to your teacher. Use the right tone of voice and facial expression.

☐ **Community**—You've been planning to have your birthday party at the skating rink. You find out the rink will be closed the week you planned to have the party. Show an optimistic attitude when you talk to your parents about it. Remember to use good body language and appropriate volume and tone of voice.

## Skill 17

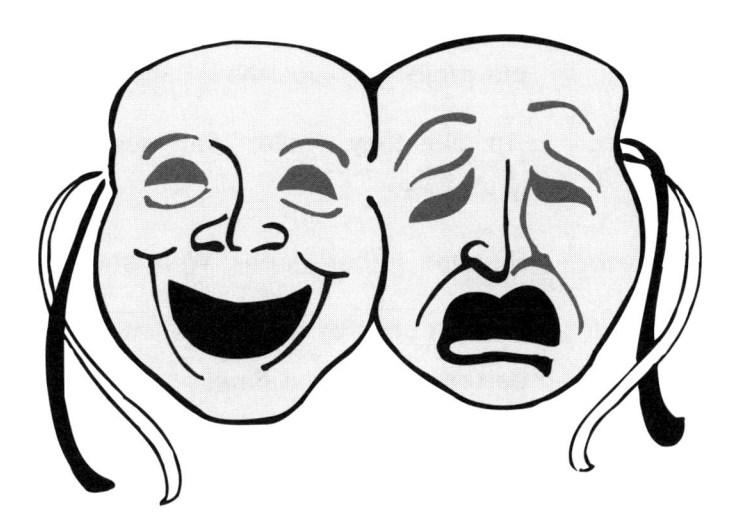

# Optimism

**Number of Characters:** 4

**Character Descriptions:** Cynthia—a student
Ramon—a student
Eric—a student
Ms. Burton—their teacher

**Scene Description:** Three friends entered their science project in the school science fair. The project that wins first place gets to go the the next level of competition. Their teacher is telling them their project came in third.

## Script A — Skill 17

# Optimism

**Ms. Burton**  It looks like your project came in third. I know you're all disappointed, but third place is quite an accomplishment. There were 34 projects, which means yours must have impressed the judges.

**Cynthia**  [Looking down] I really thought we'd win. [Looks up with a smile.] But third place isn't bad, is it?

**Ramon**  No, it isn't bad. Ours was better than 31 other projects! [Thinks a moment.] I wonder how we could do better next time.

**Eric**  Yeah, third out of 34 is pretty good, I think.

**Cynthia**  That's not bad, is it? I bet we could do better next time.

**Ramon**  Definitely. We learned a lot from it, and I really had fun working on it. I'm ready to start another one right now!

**Eric**  Me, too.

**Cynthia**  [Thoughtfully] I wonder what the judges thought about our project. Do you think they'd talk to us, Ms. Burton?

**Ms. Burton**  I'm sure they would. What questions do you want to ask them?

**Cynthia**  Hmmm. [To her friends] What should we ask?

**Ramon**  We can start by saying we want to learn how to do a better project next time.

**Eric**  That sounds good. Then what?

*Continued on next page*

## Skill 17

# Optimism—Continued

| | |
|---|---|
| CYNTHIA | Then we can ask them what they liked about our project and how we could improve, see if they have any suggestions for us. |
| RAMON | That sounds good, too. Anything else? |
| ERIC | Maybe we should thank them for talking to us. |
| CYNTHIA | Definitely. Let's go. |
| MS. BURTON | You three are showing an optimistic attitude. You're not complaining, and you're planning for the future. I'm sure the judges will be happy to talk to you. |

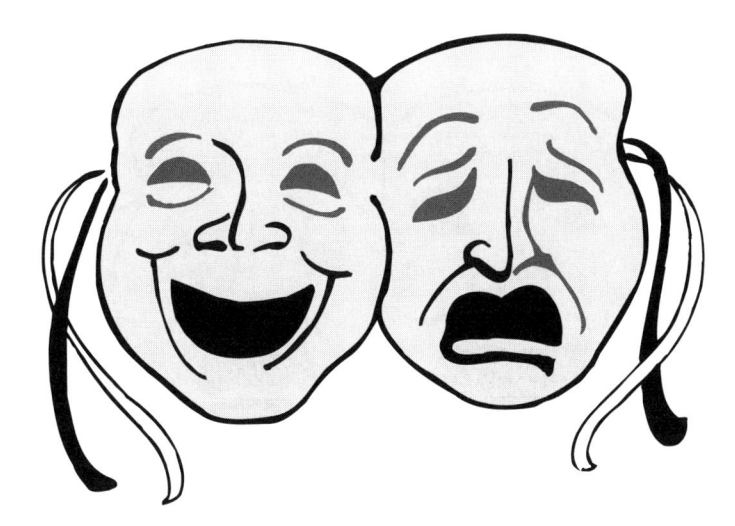

## Skill 17

# Optimism

**Number of Characters:** 3

**Character Descriptions:** Jessica–a student
Jeremy–a student
Anna–a student
Ms. Bishop–their teacher (not in the script)

**Scene Description:** Just before the end of class, Ms. Bishop has just given her students the results of their last math test. The scene begins as the students are walking to the lunchroom.

## Skill 17

# Optimism

JESSICA    [To Jeremy and Anna] **What'd you get on the math test?**

JEREMY    **I got a 78.**

ANNA    **I got an 89. I was just lucky, I guess.** [To Jessica] **What'd you get?**

JESSICA    **I got a 77. Boy, I always get bad grades in math.**

JEREMY    [Dejectedly] **Me, too. I'll never learn this stuff.**

ANNA    [Angrily] **Why do you think Ms. Bishop gives us such hard problems?**

JEREMY    **I don't know. I don't think she likes us.**

ANNA    [Fearfully] **My dad is going to be mad.**

JESSICA    **Mine, too. Not as mad as my mom, though.**

JEREMY    **Maybe my dad won't ask me about my grade.**

ANNA    [Sadly] **Mine always asks me. I never seem to get a good enough grade in math.**

JESSICA    [Being sassy] **Yeah, my mom always says, "You can do better than that." But I can't. I just don't get math.**

JEREMY    [Whining] **Now I'll probably get a bad grade on the science test, too.**

JESSICA    **Yeah, I'm not very good in science, either.**

ANNA    **I might get lucky, but I don't think so.**

JEREMY    [Angrily] **I feel like throwing my test away! Then my parents won't know how bad I am in math.**

JESSICA    [Gloomily] **I'd never get away with that. My parents would just call Ms. Bishop, and she'd tell them what I got. I guess I just have to get used to getting bad grades.** [The children continue complaining and go into the lunchroom.]

## Skill 18

# Playing Cooperatively

### Definition
Playing in a way that invites everyone to have fun.

### Activities/Discussions

1. Ask students what they think *cooperate* means. Lead them to understand it means acting together for everyone's benefit.

2. Ask students for examples of people cooperating. Write these on an overhead or on the board.

3. Have students draw a picture showing children playing cooperatively.

---

## Alternative Settings

☐ **Home**—Your cousins have come to visit. Your dad asks you to play with them while the adults get dinner ready. Show how you would play cooperatively with them.

☐ **School**—You are on the playground at recess, playing with your friends. A new student asks to join your game. Show how you would respond so everyone can have fun playing together.

☐ **Community**—You are attending a free concert in the park. You see some other children playing on the grass nearby. Show how you would ask them if you can play with them.

## Skill 18

# Playing Cooperatively

**Number of Characters:** 4

**Character Descriptions:** Cecile–a student from Alta Vista Elementary School

Raymond–a student from Alta Vista Elementary School

Jordan–a student from Fairmount Elementary School

Aaron–a student from Fairmount elementary School

**Props:** Several magnets of different sizes and shapes

**Scene Description:** Classes from different elementary schools are visiting the children's museum. At an interactive exhibit, two children from Alta Vista have begun playing with the exhibit. Two students from Fairmount walk up to the exhibit and want to join in.

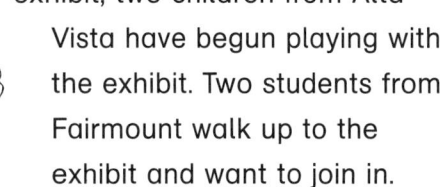

## Script A

## Skill 18

# Playing Cooperatively

| | |
|---|---|
| CECILE | [Playing with a bar magnet] **This is really neat. Watch these magnets pick this stuff up.** |
| RAYMOND | **Yeah. Let's see if these two magnets stick together.** |
| CECILE | **Wow. They won't stick together! It's really hard to even get them close! They're repelling each other.** |
| JORDAN | [Jordan and Aaron walk up to Cecile and Raymond.] **Hi. Do you mind if we play with these, too?** |
| AARON | **Those magnets look cool. Mind if we play with these two?** |
| RAYMOND | **Sure. They're really neat. These two won't stick together. They repel each other because they're magnetically the same.** |
| CECILE | **You can hardly get them close together.** |
| AARON | **Here, try it with this one.** |
| CECILE | **They stick! They must be magnetically opposite because they attract each other.** |
| JORDAN | [To Cecile] **See if yours will stick to this one.** [Holds out another bar magnet.] |
| CECILE | **These stick together, too.** |
| RAYMOND | [To Jordon] **Wonder if this one will stick to yours?** [Holds up a horseshoe magnet.] |
| AARON | [Drags his magnet through some sand.] **I don't know, but this one attracts little pieces of metal in the sand.** |

*Continued on next page*

## Skill 18
# Playing Cooperatively—Continued

**Script A**

CECILE [To Jordan and Aaron] **Raymond's and mine pick up these little pieces of metal, too. Let's see what yours pick up.**

JORDAN **Mine picks up these bottle caps, but not the plastic ones.**

AARON **Mine is picking up these needles.**

RAYMOND **This is fun! I hope we can play with magnets again when we get back to Mr. Flawn's class.**

AARON **You get to play with magnets at your school?**

CECILE **Yeah, we get to do all kinds of neat stuff in Mr. Flawn's class.** [Cecile and Raymond's teacher calls to them.]

RAYMOND **Uh, oh, we have to go. See you later. Bye!**

CECILE **Yeah, we'll see you. Bye.**

AARON AND JORDAN **Bye. Thanks for letting us play with you!**

*Peer Interaction Skills*

## Skill 18

# Playing Cooperatively

**Number of Characters:** 4

**Character Descriptions:** Three friends:
- Gerald–a boy
- Terri–a girl
- Gary–a boy

Baird–a boy the friends don't know

**Scene Description:** Three friends are at the park, playing on a playscape. The adults with the children can see the playscape but are not very close, sitting on a bench. Another child arrives at the playscape. The scene begins as this child approaches the three friends.

*Skill 18*

# Playing Cooperatively

**Script B**

GERALD  [Terri finishes crossing the monkey bars.] **Hey, Terri, you're doing great on the bars! You went all the way across.**

TERRI  **Yeah! It was my first time to get all the way across.** [To Gary, who is almost at the end of the bars] **You're almost across. Keep going; you can make it!**

BAIRD  [Starts across the bars from the other side.] **Look out! I'm coming through!**

GARY  **No, wait! I'm coming over.**

BAIRD  **Get out of my way, you twerp.** [Pushes Gary off the bars. Surprised, Gary sits on the ground.]

GERALD  **What do you think you're doing?**

BAIRD  **I'm playing here!**

TERRI  **We were here first!**

BAIRD  **So what? You don't own this park.**

TERRI  **So we were here first! You can't just barge in like that!**

BAIRD  **Says who? You? Ha! I can do whatever I want. This is a public park.**

GERALD  **C'mon, Terri. Let's go. Get up, Gary. We're leaving.**

TERRI  **Boy, he sure doesn't know how to play, does he?**

GERALD  **No. He's just a bully. Are you OK, Gary?**

GARY  **Yeah. I've just got some sand in my shoes. He was mean! What a creep!**

TERRI  **Don't worry about him. Nobody will play with him if he acts like that.**

*Skill 19*

# Respecting Differences

## Definition

Understanding that we are all unique and equally important.

## Activities/Discussions

1. Ask students for examples of ways people are unique; focus on external attributes. List the examples on an overhead or on the board.

2. Lead a discussion about how people are alike; focus on emotions and feelings.

3. Have students draw a picture of what they think respect looks like.

4. Review manners and listening basics.

---

## Alternative Settings

☐ **Home**—Your father has brought his supervisor to dinner. You are surprised to see that he has an artificial arm. Describe what you would say when you are introduced to show respect.

☐ **School**—One of your classmates makes a mean remark about another student's clothing. Describe what you could say to your classmate to show that you respect differences. Remember to calm down, think, then act.

☐ **Community**—You are walking in the mall with your friend, who wears thick eyeglasses. An older boy says something mean to her as you walk past. Describe what you would say to her to show you respect differences.

## Skill 19

# Respecting Differences

**Number of Characters:** 7

**Character Descriptions:** Mr. Ramos–the director of a soup kitchen

A family that volunteers at the soup kitchen:
- Ms. Johnson–the mother
- Mr. Johnson–the father
- Leigh Johnson–a girl
- Kenneth Johnson–a boy

James–a man in a wheelchair

Bradley–a man using a white cane

**Props:** Wheelchair for James; white cane for Bradley; chairs set up to look like a car

**Scene Description:** A family volunteers at a soup kitchen run by a local charity group. The scene begins when the volunteers begin serving food to the people who come to the kitchen. Each volunteer is responsible for dishing up one type of food as people come through the line. Some of the people going through the line wear ragged clothing. Some have physical disabilities; others have mental disabilities.

## Script A

# Skill 19
# Respecting Differences

| | |
|---|---|
| Mr. Ramos | **Hello, James. How are you tonight? Would you like some of this meatloaf? It's very good tonight.** |
| James | **Yes. I'll try it. I'll try some of those potatoes, too.** |
| Mr. Ramos | **Leigh, would you help James get these potatoes onto his plate?** |
| Leigh | **Yes, sir.** [Serves some potatoes.] **Is this enough?** |
| James | **That'll be fine. Thanks.** |
| Leigh | **You're welcome.** |
| Kenneth | **Would you like some vegetables, sir?** [Helps James scoop some vegetables.] |
| James | **Thank you.** |
| Kenneth | **You're welcome.** |
| Ms. Johnson | **This bread was just baked. Would you like two pieces?** [Puts the bread on James's plate.] |
| James | **Yes, ma'am. Thank you.** |
| Ms. Johnson | **You're most welcome.** |
| Mr. Johnson | **The dessert today is rice pudding. Would you like some?** |
| James | **Yes. Thanks.** |
| Mr. Johnson | [Puts pudding on James's plate.] **Certainly!** |
| Mr. Ramos | **Hello, Bradley. How are you today?** |
| Bradley | **I'm doing pretty good today.** |
| Mr. Ramos | **Glad to hear it. How about some meatloaf? It's very tasty today.** |

*Continued on next page*

## Skill 19

# Respecting Differences—Continued

| | |
|---|---|
| BRADLEY | **OK, that sounds good.** |
| LEIGH | **Hello. Would you like some potatoes, too?** |
| BRADLEY | **Um hm.** [Leigh puts potatoes on Bradley's plate.] **Thanks. What are those vegetables I heard about?** |
| KENNETH | **We have carrots, squash, and green beans. May I serve you some?** |
| BRADLEY | **Yes.** [Kenneth puts vegetables on Bradley's plate.] |
| MS. JOHNSON | **Would you like some bread, too?** |
| BRADLEY | **Yes, ma'am.** |
| MS. JOHNSON | **One or two slices?** |
| BRADLEY | **Two, please.** [Ms. Johnson puts two slices on his plate.] |
| | [The family finishes serving food and gets into the car. On the way home, they talk about their experiences.] |
| MR. JOHNSON | **Kenneth, I am very proud of how polite you were to James and Bradley tonight. I sure admire the way James gets around in his wheelchair. He must be strong to go up and down those ramps.** |
| KENNETH | **I found out last week he builds model airplanes.** |
| MR. JOHNSON | **No kidding!** |
| KENNETH | **No kidding. I'd really like to see them sometime. I wonder if he'd bring them next week.** |

## Skill 19

# Respecting Differences

**Number of Characters:** 4

**Character Descriptions:** Three friends:
- Sima—a girl
- Carolyn—a girl
- Brian—a boy

Gail—a woman with an artificial leg

**Scene Description:** The three friends are swimming in the park swimming pool. Gail comes through the gate, sits down on the edge of the pool, removes her artificial leg, and slips into the water.

*Skill 19*

# Respecting Differences

**Script B**

| | |
|---|---|
| SIMA | **Look at that lady! She took her leg off!** |
| CAROLYN | **Oh, gross! I can't even look at her.** |
| BRIAN | **Eee-ooh! It's on the ledge! Don't go near it!** |
| SIMA | **What's wrong with you two?** |
| CAROLYN | **I'm getting out of here.** |

[The children swim to the other end of the pool and whisper to each other. Gail swims nearby.]

| | |
|---|---|
| BRIAN | **Hey, lady! Can we see your leg?** |
| GAIL | **Sure, I'll show it to you.** |
| CAROLYN | **Brian! What are you doing? I'm not going over there!** |
| SIMA | **I am.** |
| BRIAN | [To Carolyn] **You scaredy cat! It won't bite you.** |

[Sima and Brian swim over to Gail. She shows them her artificial leg.]

| | |
|---|---|
| BRIAN | **What happened to your real leg?** |
| GAIL | **I lost it in an accident when I was a girl.** |
| BRIAN | **That must have been a long time ago.** |
| GAIL | [Laughs.] **Yes, it was.** |

[Brian and Sima go back to Carolyn.]

| | |
|---|---|
| BRIAN | **She's so old. I don't see how she can even walk with that thing.** |

*Continued on next page*

*Peer Interaction Skills*

## Skill 19

# Respecting Differences—*Continued*

SIMA    Brian, you don't know how to appreciate when people are different from you. How would you feel if somebody talked about you like that?

BRIAN    Like what?

SIMA    What if they said your black hair was ugly?

BRIAN    Nobody would say that! Besides, my hair is just fine!

SIMA    They might! And then how would you feel?

BRIAN    I'd hit them.

SIMA    But how would you feel? Wouldn't you feel bad if someone said your hair was ugly?

BRIAN    I guess so.

SIMA    That's what I mean. That lady would feel bad if she knew what you were saying about her. Besides, having an artificial leg doesn't mean she doesn't have any feelings, or that she's stupid.

CAROLYN    How do you know?

SIMA    We did a unit in class on respecting differences. We learned that people are more alike than different, and that external differences aren't that important.

*Skill 20*

# Being a Friend

## Definition
Choosing words and actions that show someone you care.

## Activities/Discussions
1. Ask students what makes a friend; list their ideas on an overhead or on the board.

2. Lead a discussion about the ways friends show each other they care. List ideas under the headings of *words* and *actions*.

3. Have students list the qualities they would like in an ideal friend. Reinforce earlier skill units.

---

## Alternative Settings

☐ **Home**—Your friend is visiting you at your house. Demonstrate how you would show her that you care about her.

☐ **School**—In the hallway after school you see an older student picking on a younger student. Show how you would act like a friend to the younger student. Remember to calm down, think, then act.

☐ **Community**—You are at the park with your friend and his younger brother. The younger brother falls off a swing and begins to cry. Show what you would do and say to show him you care.

## Skill 20

# Being a Friend

**Number of Characters:** 4

**Character Descriptions:** Clifton—a boy
Brandye—a girl
Sara—a girl
Mr. Washington—Sara's dad

**Scene Description:** Clifton, Brandye, and Sara are playing ball in Sara's yard. Last week, Sara's brother hit a ball through one of the windows in the house. The window has just been replaced.

## Skill 20

# Being a Friend

**Script A**

SARA — **Pitch it right here, Brandye.**

BRANDYE — **OK. Here it comes.**

[Sara hits the ball. It flies into the window and breaks it.]

CLIFTON — **Uh, oh! It's broken!**

BRANDYE — **Oh, boy! It sure is!**

SARA — **Oh, no. I don't believe this. My dad will be furious.**

CLIFTON — **Why?**

SARA — **He just fixed this window. He made my brother pay for it, too. I don't have enough in my allowance to pay for it.**

BRANDYE — **Let's calm down and think. We'll help you, won't we, Clifton? I have $7.00**

CLIFTON — **Yeah. I have $4.00.**

[Mr. Washington drives into the driveway. He gets out of the car.]

MR. WASHINGTON — [Friendly] **Hi, kids. What're you up to?**

SARA — **Uh, Dad, you're not going to like this.**

MR. WASHINGTON — [Worried] **Uh, oh. I can tell I'm not. What is it?**

SARA — **I broke the window.**

MR. WASHINGTON — **The window? The same window?**

SARA — **Yes. I didn't mean to! I hit it wrong, I guess, and it flew right through the window.**

*Continued on next page* ➡

*Peer Interaction Skills*

## Skill 20

# Being a Friend—Continued

| | |
|---|---|
| MR. WASHINGTON | You know you'll have to pay for it. |
| SARA | I know. |
| CLIFTON | We'll help, Mr. Washington. I have $4.00. |
| SARA | I have $8.00. |
| BRANDYE | And I have $7.00. How much will a new window cost? |
| MR. WASHINGTON | Nineteen dollars will cover most of the cost, and I can install it myself. You two are sure good friends to help Sara like this. |
| SARA | Yeah! You're both good friends. Thanks a lot. |
| CLIFTON | You're welcome, Sara. |
| BRANDYE | Sure. I hope we don't break any other windows for awhile. I was saving my allowance to get my mom a birthday present. Maybe from now on we should play baseball at the park! |
| SARA | I'll pay you back, Brandye. As soon as I have $7.00, I'll give it to you. And I'll pay you back, too, Clifton. |
| MR. WASHINGTON | [To Brandye and Clifton] **Sara is lucky to have such good friends**. [Turns to Sara.] Maybe we can work it out so you don't have to use your friends' money. We can talk about it when we go get a new window. Thank you for telling the truth and having a positive attitude. |

## Skill 20

# Being a Friend

**Number of Characters:**  3

**Character Descriptions:**  Three friends:
- Adrian—a boy
- Yvonne—a girl
- Lincoln—a boy

**Scene Description:**  The three friends are late arriving home from school because they stopped to talk to another friend on the playground and lost track of the time.

# Skill 20

# Being a Friend

ADRIAN    Oh, no! I'm late. My mom is going to be mad.

YVONNE    Why?

ADRIAN    She told me to be home by 3:15 today so we could go pick up my sister.

LINCOLN    Why do you have to go with her?

ADRIAN    Because we're going over to my aunt's for dinner. Will you come inside to help me tell her why we were late?

YVONNE    No, I can't. I have to go now.

ADRIAN    But you're not late! You could stay to talk to my mom with me.

YVONNE    Not me. I'm going home to watch TV. You'll just have to talk to her yourself.

[Adrian starts toward her house. Lincoln stays a moment to talk to Yvonne.]

LINCOLN    Yvonne, why can't you help Adrian talk to her mom?

YVONNE    She doesn't need our help. She can talk to her mom by herself. I'm not helping her.

LINCOLN    You're not being a very good friend.

YVONNE    What do you mean?

LINCOLN    A good friend would help Adrian talk to her mom. We were all responsible for her being late.

*Continued on next page*

## *Skill 20*
# Being a Friend—*Continued*

**Script B**

YVONNE     **Well, it's not my fault she's late. I'm going home.**

LINCOLN     **Well, I'm going to help her talk to her mom.** [Runs to catch up with Adrian.] **Adrian, wait! I'll help you.**

ADRIAN     [Surprised] **Gee, thanks, Lincoln. You're a good friend.**

## Skill 21

# Giving & Receiving a Compliment

### Definition
Saying something sincerely nice about another person. Thanking someone who says something sincerely nice about you.

### Activities/Discussions

1. Ask students what they think a compliment is. List their ideas on an overhead or on the board.

2. Lead a discussion about receiving and giving compliments. List ideas on an overhead or on the board under *giving compliments* and *receiving compliments*.

3. Discuss how you can tell when someone is being sincere. List students' ideas on an overhead or on the board.

------------------------------------------------------------

## Alternative Settings

☐ **Home**—Your mother has just told the family that she's been promoted at work. Compliment her on her achievement.

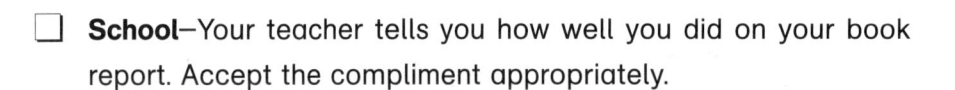

☐ **School**—Your teacher tells you how well you did on your book report. Accept the compliment appropriately.

☐ **Community**—Your friend just finished a three-mile fundraising walk for a local charity. Compliment him for finishing the walk.

## Skill 21

# Giving & Receiving a Compliment

**Number of Characters:** 4

**Character Descriptions:** Grant–a boy
Stephanie–a girl
Jarrell–a boy
Mitchell–a boy

**Scene Description:** Grant's recycling poster has won first place in a citywide competition for his grade level. Mitchell is an older student whose poster has won for his grade level. After the awards ceremony, Grant's friends are congratulating him.

## Script A

# Skill 21
# Giving & Receiving a Compliment

STEPHANIE   Wow, Grant. Your poster is really terrific. Congratulations.

JARRELL   Yeah, it's awesome. You really did a great job. I liked the colors you used; they're bright and eye-catching.

GRANT   Thank you. Thanks a lot. Yours was really good, too, Stephanie.

STEPHANIE   Oh, thanks. I thought it was pretty good. Not as good as yours, though. You really deserved to win. Jarrell's right. The colors you used really stand out.

GRANT   Thanks. I'm just surprised I won. Jarrell, I liked your poster, too. I know you worked hard on it.

JARRELL   Yeah, I did. My mom helped me, too. But yours was the best. You have a true talent for this, Grant.

GRANT   Thank you both. You're great friends. [Sees Mitchell across the room.] Oh, there's Mitchell. I want to tell him what a great job he did, too. [Walks up to Mitchell.] Hi, Mitchell. Congratulations! Your poster is really good.

MITCHELL   Oh, hi, Grant. Thank you. Didn't you win, too?

GRANT   Yeah. I got first place in my grade.

MITCHELL   Way to go! I thought your poster looked terrific.

GRANT   Gee, thanks, Mitchell. It means a lot to me for you to say that. I hope I get as good as you are.

MITCHELL   You're already good. Just keep working at it. The more you paint, the better you'll get.

*Continued on next page*

## Skill 21

# Giving & Receiving a Compliment—*Continued*

GRANT    I will. Well, see you, Mitchell.

MITCHELL    OK. See you later, Grant.

[Grant walks back to his friends.]

GRANT    Boy, he sure made me feel good.

JARRELL    What'd he say?

GRANT    He told me how good my poster was.

STEPHANIE    I bet all this makes you happy.

GRANT    Yeah, with you two as friends, and with Mitchell encouraging me about my poster, I feel terrific!

## Skill 21

# Giving & Receiving a Compliment

**Number of Characters:** 3

**Character Descriptions:** Dr. Evers–superintendent of schools
Martin–a student
Maria–a student

**Scene Description:** Martin and Maria have won the top spots in the citywide spelling bee. They are meeting with the superintendent of schools after the awards ceremony.

# Skill 21
# Giving & Receiving a Compliment

**Script B**

DR. EVERS — Congratulations on your excellent spelling, you two. You must have worked very hard to get this far.

MARTIN — Thank you, Dr. Evers.

MARIA — Oh, I wasn't that good. I didn't think I was going to win. I was just lucky.

DR. EVERS — How did you study to learn the words?

MARTIN — My parents helped me every day. And my sister helped, too. We went through every spelling list we could find.

MARIA — My dad helped me.

DR. EVERS — Congratulations again. I know you'll both do well in the state finals.

MARTIN — Thank you. I hope so, too.

MARIA — [Looks down and shuffles her feet.] I'll probably lose in the first round. I almost lost today.

DR. EVERS — I disagree, Maria. Nobody wins the citywide tournament by accident. You'll do just fine when you get to the finals.

[Dr. Evers goes to talk to their parents.]

MARTIN — Dr. Evers made me feel great. Knowing she's behind us makes me believe I can win the state finals.

MARIA — I'm too scared. I don't think I'll make it past the first round. I'll probably embarrass everybody by missing the very first word.

MARTIN — No way! With all the support we've got, I know we can do well.

## Skill 22

# Building a Positive Reputation

### Definition
Making responsible choices that invite others to have positive thoughts about you.

### Activities/Discussions

1. Ask students for examples of characters with a bad reputation (e.g., the wolf in *The Three Little Pigs*; Grim Snake-in-the-Grass in *Viking It and Liking It,* by Jon Scieszka; Bad Guy in *Bill and Pete to the Rescue,* by Tomie dePaola; or Draco Malfoy in the *Harry Potter* series by J.K. Rowlings). Discuss what the character did or said to deserve the bad reputation.

2. Brainstorm with students a list of actions and words that invite others to have positive thoughts about a person (i.e., build a positive reputation). List them on an overhead or on the board under actions and words.

3. Divide students into pairs. Have the pairs use the lists to decide which actions go with which words. Ask each group to report on their decisions.

------

## Alternative Settings

☐ **Home**—Your older brother has many friends and is frequently asked to do things with them. Ask him what he has done and said to build his positive reputation.

☐ **School**—Some of the students in your school treat the cafeteria workers in a mean way. Show what you would do and say to build a positive reputation with them.

☐ **Community**—You and your family belong to a volunteer group that is having a potluck dinner meeting. During the cleanup afterwards, use actions and words to build a positive reputation.

## Skill 22

# Building a Positive Reputation

**Number of Characters:** 7

**Character Descriptions:**
Calvin–a boy
Alisa–a girl
Kyla–a girl
Maurice–a boy
Mr. Kidder–Alisa's father
Ms. Holland–Alisa's mother
Narrator

**Props:** Chairs set up like a movie theater

**Scene Description:** Four friends have gone to a movie with Alisa's parents. Their parents have agreed that the friends can sit by themselves in the theater. The scene begins before the movie has started, when advertisements are showing on the screen.

## Script A

# Skill 22
# Building a Positive Reputation

| | |
|---|---|
| Ms. Holland | **Remember what we talked about? You're going to be quiet during the movie. If you talk, people will think you're rude.** |
| Mr. Kidder | **You can show how to be respectful of other people.** |
| Maurice | **OK, Ms. Holland. We won't talk.** |
| Alisa | **We won't talk, Dad. But we can talk until the previews begin, right, Mom?** |
| Ms. Holland | **Right.** |
| Calvin | **Don't worry, Mr. Kidder. We'll be quiet.** |
| Kyla | **Yeah, we'll be quiet, Ms. Holland.** |
| Narrator | **[The friends sit down and begin watching the advertisements.]** |
| Calvin | **That was cool. I like the way the two moose talk to the audience.** |
| Alisa | **They're pretty funny.** |
| Kyla | **They sound dumb to me.** |
| Maurice | **No way! They're cool.** |
| Alisa | **They're just so . . . I don't know. They make me laugh.** |
| Calvin | **Yeah, me too. Hey, you want some popcorn?** |
| Kyla | **Sure. Thanks, Calvin.** |
| Alisa | **Yeah, thanks Calvin.** |
| Narrator | **[The previews begin.]** |

*Continued on next page*

## Skill 22

# Building a Positive Reputation—*Continued*

| | |
|---|---|
| CALVIN | [Whispers.] **Kyla, pass some over here.** |
| KYLA | [Whispers.] **Here.** |
| MAURICE | [Whispers.] **Pass it here, Calvin.** |
| CALVIN | [Whispers.] **Here.** |
| ALISA | [Whispers.] **We should be quiet now.** |
| KYLA | [Whispers.] **Yeah. We don't want people to think we're rude.** [Whispers.] **Calvin, here's your popcorn.** |
| NARRATOR | [Once the movie begins, the children watch without talking. When the movie ends, they get up and join Alisa's parents.] |
| MR. KIDDER | **I'm really proud of you kids. You were quiet during the whole movie. Way to go!** |
| MS. HOLLAND | **Yes. Nice job. The people next to us said what great kids you were. We told them you were with us!** |

## Skill 22

# Building a Positive Reputation

**Number of Characters:** 4

**Character Descriptions:** Akiko–a student
Ms. Lee–Akiko's mother
Jenny–a student
Ms. White–Jenny's mother

**Scene Description:** Akiko and her mother see Jenny and her mother while they are walking in the mall. They stop to talk.

## Skill 22

# Building a Positive Reputation

**Script B**

| | |
|---|---|
| AKIKO | **Hi, Jenny.** |
| JENNY | **Oh, hi, Akiko.** |
| MS. LEE | **Hello, Ms. White. How are you?** |
| MS. WHITE | **Fine. How are you?** |
| | [The girls' mothers begin talking to each other.] |
| AKIKO | **What are you shopping for?** |
| JENNY | [Looks at people walking past and doesn't answer.] |
| AKIKO | **I'm looking for a jacket. My mom is helping me find one I can wear to school.** |
| JENNY | [Doesn't say anything. Looks at her feet.] |
| AKIKO | **What did you do for your history project?** |
| JENNY | **I did a diary of a pioneer girl.** |
| AKIKO | **That sounds interesting. Who did you choose?** |
| JENNY | **Sallie Fox.** |
| AKIKO | **Oh, we learned about her, too. Isn't she the one in Iowa?** |
| JENNY | **Yeah.** [Sees someone she knows and leaves to talk to her.] |
| | [Ms. White and Ms. Lee turn to Akiko.] |
| MS. WHITE | **Where did Jenny go?** |
| AKIKO | **Oh, she's just over there.** [Points to Jenny.] |

*Continued on next page*

## Skill 22

# Building a Positive Reputation—*Continued*

**Script B**

MS. LEE  **Well, it was nice to see you, Ms. White. Goodbye.**

MS. WHITE  **Goodbye! I hope to see you again soon.** [She walks toward Jenny.]

[Akiko and her mother walk toward a shop.]

MS. LEE  **I noticed that Jenny didn't seem very friendly. Did she even say anything to you?**

AKIKO  **She barely said two words. She saw someone else she knew and then she just walked away like I wasn't even there. She didn't even excuse herself. How rude!**

MS. LEE  **I agree. It's hard to be her friend if she behaves like that. That's no way to build a positive reputation and make good friends.**

## Skill 23
# Dealing with Teasing

### Definition
Knowing that mean teasing is not OK. Using positive strategies to stop the teasing cycle.

### Activities/Discussions

1. Ask the students what they think *teasing* means. Help them differentiate between mean teasing and friendly teasing.

2. Ask the students for examples of mean teasing, and list them on an overhead or on the board.

3. Brainstorm with the students what they can do to stop mean teasing. List their examples on an overhead or on the board under these two headings:

    - Being teased
    - Observing someone else being teased

4. Reinforce the four strategies from cognitive planning.

---

## Alternative Settings

☐ **Home**—Your older sister calls you "goofy" in front of your friends. Show how you can respond to her teasing. Remember to calm down, think, then act, then ask yourself, "What happened?"

☐ **School**—Your friends call you "egghead" because you won the schoolwide spelling championship. Show what you can do or say to stop their teasing.

☐ **Community**—You are going on a field trip to the local newspaper with your class. On the street outside the newspaper, a teenager passing by says, "You babies." Show what you would do or say.

# Skill 23

# Dealing with Teasing

**Number of Characters:** 6

**Character Descriptions:** Rosa–a student
Ann–a student
Carol–a student
Nick–a student
Joe–a student
Narrator

**Scene Description:** Rosa, Ann, and Carol are playing ball on the playground. Nick and Joe come over and start teasing them.

## Skill 23

# Dealing with Teasing

*Script A*

ROSA     [To Ann] **Kick it over here. Then I'll kick it to Carol.**

ANN     **OK. Here it comes.**

NARRATOR     [The ball goes past Rosa.]

ROSA     **Oops!**

NARRATOR     [Rosa runs to get the ball and kicks it to Carol.]

CAROL     [To Rosa] **Good kick.** [To Ann] **Here, Ann.**

NARRATOR     [Carol kicks the ball toward Ann. Ann runs up to the ball and kicks it toward Rosa. Rosa misses it and runs to get it.]

NICK     [To Rosa] **Boy, are you terrible! You can't even stop the ball. Butterfingers!**

JOE     [Laughs at Rosa.] **No wonder nobody chooses you to be on their team.**

ROSA     [To Ann and Carol] **C'mon. Let's go play somewhere else.**

NARRATOR     [The three girls pick up their ball and start walking away from the boys.]

NICK     [To Joe] **They're so bad, they have to leave!**

JOE     [To the girls] **You're afraid we're better than you! You can't stand the heat!**

ROSA     [To the other two girls] **Let's just keep walking and ignore them.**

ANN     **Yeah, ignoring them is the best.**

*Continued on next page*

## Skill 23

# Dealing with Teasing—Continued

**Script A**

| | |
|---|---|
| JOE | [In a singsong voice] **Rosa! Rosa! Come back so we can watch you miss the ball!** |
| CAROL | **Don't say anything to them. They'll just keep it up.** |
| ROSA | **I wouldn't mind if they wanted to play. But they just want to make fun of us.** |
| NICK | **Carol! Come back!** |
| CAROL | **Let's just pretend we don't hear them.** |
| ANN | **Good idea. They'll just keep it up if we pay attention to them.** [The girls keep walking away from the boys.] |
| NICK | **Hey, where are they going? They don't want to listen to us.** |
| JOE | **I don't know. I guess we're not going to get their attention.** |

## Skill 23

# Dealing with Teasing

**Setting B**

**Number of Characters:** 5

**Character Descriptions:** Otis–a student
Louis–a student
Perry–a student
Leland–a student
Ms. Parker–Otis's mother

**Scene Description:** The four boys are putting on their swim trunks to go play outside in the lawn sprinkler. Otis, Louis, and Perry are teasing Leland about his trunks.

Peer Interaction Skills

123

## Skill 23

# Dealing with Teasing

| | |
|---|---|
| OTIS | [Pointing to Leland's swim trunks.] **Look at those funny trunks!** |
| LOUIS | **They're ridiculous! You look like a flower!** |
| LELAND | **Shut up, Louis!** |
| PERRY | **What's wrong, Leland? Aren't you a flower?** |
| LELAND | **I'm not a flower!** |
| OTIS | [In a singsong voice] **Flower, flower! Leland is a flower!** |
| LOUIS | [In a singsong voice] **Leland is a flower!** |
| PERRY | **He's a flower and doesn't know it!** |
| LELAND | **Will you shut up! I am not a flower!** |
| MS. PARKER | [Comes into the room.] **What's going on here?** |
| LELAND | [Looks at the other boys.] **Nothing. We're just getting ready to go outside.** |
| MS. PARKER | **What's going on, Otis? It sounded like more than nothing to me.** |
| OTIS | **Oh, we were just teasing Leland about his swim trunks. We didn't mean anything.** |
| MS. PARKER | **Is that right, Leland?** |
| LELAND | **Yes, ma'am.** |

*Continued on next page*

## Skill 23

# Dealing with Teasing—Continued

| | |
|---|---|
| Ms. Parker | I heard what you were saying. You weren't just teasing Leland. You were mean about it. Leland, what could you do to stop them from teasing you in a mean way? |
| Leland | I don't know. |
| Ms. Parker | You can ignore them. Then they'll stop. |
| Leland | It's hard. |
| Ms. Parker | I know, but that's what you have to do. Or you could just walk away from them. Do you think that might work? Will you try that? |
| Leland | Yes, ma'am, I'll try. |
| Ms. Parker | And, you boys need to stop that teasing. You all know better than that. |
| Otis, Louis, and Perry | Yes, ma'am. |
| Ms. Parker | Otis, do you remember what you learned about mean teasing? |
| Otis | Yes, ma'am. |
| Ms. Parker | What did you learn? |
| Otis | I learned that mean teasing is not OK because it's not respectful. It hurts people's feelings. |
| Ms. Parker | That's right. I hope you'll remember that from now on. |

*Skill 24*

# Getting into a Group

**Staging**

## Definition

Moving in a positive way to form a team to work with.

## Activities/Discussions

1. Ask the students positive things they could do and say to get into their group or team. Write their ideas on an overhead or on the board under the headings *actions* and *words*.

2. Brainstorm with students ways they can show they are willing to work with whoever is in their group. Elicit ideas about words, facial expressions, and body language that illustrate their willingness.

3. Lead a discussion about the manner in which the students can move to get in their group. Focus the discussion on moving quickly and quietly to their group.

------

## Alternative Settings

- **Home**—Your older sister works in several different teams at school. Tell her your ideas about positive ways of getting into a group. Ask her if she can add any other ideas.

- **School**—Your math teacher has assigned you to a team with two students new to your class. Show how you will move in a positive way to join the team.

- **Community**—Your family is attending a picnic with several other families. Your mother tells you and your sister to sit at a table with several other children you don't know. Show how you will move in a positive way to join the group.

## Skill 24

# Getting into a Group

**Number of Characters:** 4

**Character Descriptions:** Jorgé–a student
Mickey–a student
Danny–a student
Mr. Patterson–the director of a volunteer program

**Scene Description:** Mr. Patterson, the director of a volunteer program, is assigning students to groups based on their volunteer assignments. He has asked them to number off from one to five. Jorgé, Mickey, and Danny are threes. They haven't met before.

NOTE: For more information on Habitat for Humanity, go to: http://www.habitat.org. Follow the link to "Get Involved," then "Find Local Affiliates" and "Youth & Habitat." If your community does not have a local chapter of Habitat for Humanity, you might also want to have your students discuss other ways they can volunteer.

## Skill 24

# Getting into a Group

**Script A**

| MR. PATTERSON | **We need five groups. Ones go here** [Points.], **twos go here** [Points.], **threes go here** [Points.], **fours go here** [Points.], **and fives go here** [Points.]. |
| --- | --- |
| | [The three boys walk quickly and quietly to their groups.] |
| JORGÉ | [Smiles at Mickey and Danny.] **Hello. My name is Jorgé.** |
| MICKEY | [Smiles.] **Hi, Jorgé. My name is Michael. But everybody calls me Mickey.** |
| JORGÉ | **Hi, Mickey.** |
| DANNY | [Smiles at Jorgé and Mickey.] **Hi, my name is Danny. Nice to know you.** |
| MICKEY | **I wonder what our assignment will be? Do you know?** |
| JORGÉ | **My brother did this last year. He got to go to Habitat for Humanity.** |
| MICKEY | **Oh, I've heard about them. What did your brother do there?** |
| JORGÉ | **He got to help in the office and in the warehouse.** |
| DANNY | **What did he do? Did he get to drive the forklift?** |
| JORGÉ | [Laughs.] **No, he wanted to, but the foreman told him he was too young.** [Pauses.] **In the warehouse, he helped the warehouse lady write stuff down. In the office, he filed documents and told people where to take donations.** |

*Continued on next page*

*Skill 24*

# Getting into a Group—*Continued*

**Script A**

| | |
|---|---|
| DANNY | That sounds fun. |
| MICKEY | I wonder what some of the other assignments are. |
| MR. PATTERSON | [Walks over to the threes.] You threes are going to volunteer at the assisted-living center. |
| JORGÉ | What will we do there? |
| MR. PATTERSON | You'll talk to the people who live there. |
| DANNY | [In a scared voice] What will we say? |
| MR. PATTERSON | I'd like you to work together right now to think of topics you can talk about. Your first visit is tomorrow. |
| MICKEY | I know how to talk to older people. My great grandmother lives in an assisted place. I like visiting her there. |
| JORGÉ | You sound like you know what to do. [Pulls out a sheet of paper and a pencil.] Let's get started. |
| DANNY | Yes, let's get started. I think I'm going to like this! |

*Peer Interaction Skills*

# Skill 24

# Getting into a Group

**Number of Characters:** 7

**Character Descriptions:** Ms. Philllips—the art teacher

Students:
- Akil
- Julie
- Brian
- Sean
- Kaitlin
- Caroline (not in the script)
- Jessica (not in the script)

Narrator

**Props:** Overhead; chalkboard or poster

**Scene Description:** As part of a schoolwide theme on oceans, Ms. Phillips's art class is working on a mural for the hallway next to the office. She has divided the class into five groups, which she has posted on an overhead. Each group will design one section of the mural. The scene begins just after the students have entered her classroom and taken their seats.

## Skill 24

# Getting into a Group

**Script B**

MS. PHILLIPS — Today we're going to start on the mural project. I've assigned everyone to a group. [Points to the assignments on the overhead, chalkboard, or poster.] **I want each group to come up with an idea of what they're going to do for the mural. I'll come around to help you think of what you want to do. Get in your groups now.**

AKIL — [Whispers to Brian.] **I don't want to be in the group with Caroline and Jessica.**

BRIAN — [Whispers to Akil.] **Me either. They're too serious about drawing.**

MS. PHILLIPS — [Walks up to Akil and Brian.] **Akil, Brian, let's hear what you have to say.**

AKIL — **I don't want to be in that group.**

BRIAN — **I don't, either. Can we change groups?**

MS. PHILLIPS — **No, this is the group you're in for this project. Time to move over there now.**

NARRATOR — [Akil and Brian get up slowly. Akil goes to sharpen his pencil. Brian follows him. Then they stop to look out the window. Julie and Kaitlin, who are in the same group as the two boys, walk up to Akil and Brian.]

JULIE — **Nobody will want to be in your group if you're not willing to work with them.**

AKIL — **What do you mean?**

*Continued on next page* →

*Peer Interaction Skills*

## Skill 24

# Getting into a Group—Continued

**Script B**

| KAITLIN | You make people feel bad when you say you don't want to be in their group. |
|---|---|
| BRIAN | I don't care. I don't want to be in that group. |
| JULIE | What if somebody said the same thing about you? |
| AKIL | I wouldn't like it. |
| JULIE | How would you feel, Brian? |
| BRIAN | [Thinks a minute.] I guess I wouldn't like it, either. |
| NARRATOR | [The four students start toward their group. Ms. Phillips watches them and decides they're beginning to solve their problem on their own.] |
| KAITLIN | I know I wouldn't like it if you said you didn't want to be in my group. |
| BRIAN | I wouldn't say that about you. |
| KAITLIN | I know. Still, Caroline and Jessica probably think you don't like them. |
| AKIL | What should I say to them? |
| JULIE | Maybe you could just say you're sorry you said that. |
| AKIL | Yeah, I don't want them to think I don't like them. I just think they're too serious about drawing. |
| BRIAN | They make me look bad in art class! |
| KAITLIN | Well, maybe we'll learn something from them! They could make our good ideas look even better! |
| BRIAN | I sure hope so! |

## Skill 25

# Giving Put-Ups

## Definition
Inviting all group members to feel positive.

## Activities/Discussions
1. Ask students for one example of a put-down. Then ask them what they think the opposite of a put-down is.

2. Ask students for examples of "put-ups" they can use in their groups. List them on an overhead or on the board.

3. Have students draw a picture of someone who's just received a put-down and a picture of someone who's just received a put-up.

4. Review cognitive strategies.

---

## Alternative Settings

☐ **Home**—Your sister is having a difficult time with a homework assignment. Use a put-up to encourage her.

☐ **School**—One of your group members made a mistake on the assignment. Give her or him an appropriate put-up. Remember to calm down, think, then act. Then ask yourself, "What happened?"

☐ **Community**—You are eating in a restaurant with your friend and her or his family. Her/his little sister is just learning to read and is excited when she discovers she can read some of the items on the menu. Give her an appropriate put-up.

*Skill 25*

# Giving Put-Ups

**Setting A**

**Number of Characters:** 6

**Character Descriptions:** Mr. Mackey—the social studies teacher

Student group members:
- Ji-Eun
- Tabitha
- Jack
- Natalie
- Tomas

**Props:** Drawings; pictures

**Scene Description:** As part of a social studies unit on Native Americans who live near oceans, Mr. Mackey's class is working on group projects about the types of food they eat. The groups have been doing research for two weeks and are now ready to start on the report they will make to the entire class. This group has been studying nutrition among first nations in the Pacific Northwest.

NOTE: you may have to adapt this script if your students have not studied oceans.

*Peer Interaction Skills*

## Skill 25

# Giving Put-Ups

JI-EUN    OK, we have to decide what we want to have in our report.

TABITHA    I think we should have pictures of the kinds of food they eat. I found these pictures on the Internet. [Shows pictures of smoked salmon, smoked eulachon, herring eggs on kelp, clams, and dried seaweed.]

JACK    Way to go, Tabitha! These pictures really show what their food looks like. Everything looks almost real.

JI-EUN    Yeah, great job, Tabitha. These will help a lot.

JACK    I've drawn some of the people at a conference on nutrition. Maybe we can use them to show what the people look like.

NATALIE    Do you mean show how they look when they eat a certain diet?

JACK    Yeah. When Tabitha told us about how they ate herring eggs on kelp, I was curious what they would look like. Do you think they look different from us?

TOMAS    I never thought of that. If you eat different things, do you look different? Let's see your drawings, Jack.

[Jack shows the group his drawings.]

TOMAS    They look just like us! [Smiles.] I guess eating herring eggs doesn't affect how you look! I wonder how I'd look if I ate horny-toad tails?

JI-EUN    Ick! That sounds terrible, Tomas! Your drawings are cool, Jack. Can we copy them for everybody, or should we put them on an overhead?

*Continued on next page*

**Script A**

# Skill 25

# Giving Put-Ups—Continued

| | |
|---|---|
| NATALIE | Let's ask Mr. Mackey if we can copy them. They're really cool, Jack. Tomas, you're the best writer. Can you write down what we should say? |
| TOMAS | Sure! We can all practice what we want to say, and I'll write it down so we'll have it for our report. |
| JACK | Oh, good! Thanks, Tomas. |
| NATALIE | I'm having trouble figuring out how to put their foods into the food pyramid. I'm not sure what some of these things are, so I have to look everything up. Like eulachon. I had to look it up to find out it's a kind of fish. |
| TOMAS | Don't worry, Natalie. You're doing a great job. If you need help looking things up, we can help you with it. |
| TABITHA | Yeah, don't worry, Natalie. I'm finished finding stuff on their nutrition and dental health, so I can help you, too. |
| NATALIE | Thanks, everyone. I feel much better now. I was really worried I wouldn't get finished in time. |
| JI-EUN | [To the group] While you're helping Natalie look up these foods, I can make a concept map we can follow. |
| NATALIE | Good. You know how to make concept maps the best, Ji-Eun. |
| TOMAS | Your concept maps always work, Ji-Eun. If I have your map, I won't have any trouble writing this down. |
| JACK | They're right, Ji-Eun. Your concept maps are always clear and easy to follow. |
| | [The students continue working together.] |
| MR. MACKEY | Time's up for today, everyone. Tomorrow you'll have time to get all your material on the computer. Clear your tables and get ready to go outside for recess. |

## Skill 25

# Giving Put-Ups

**Number of Characters:** 6

**Character Descriptions:** Student group members:
- Seeoowo
- Ana
- Joseph
- Catherine
- Madison
- Spencer

**Scene Description:** The class has just finished working on group projects. Each week, a different group gets to choose the Friday free-time activity. The scene begins as the students in the group choosing the activity begin discussing which activity to choose.

## Skill 25

# Giving Put-Ups

**Script B**

| | |
|---|---|
| SEEOOWO | Ana, which activity do you think we should choose? |
| ANA | [Turns to Joseph, meanly.] **Nothing you'd like, that's for sure.** |
| JOSEPH | [Sarcastically] **Thanks, Ana. You're so helpful to tell me that.** [To the others] **I'm not sure which one I want.** |
| CATHERINE | Madison, which one do you want to choose? |
| MADISON | Oh, I don't know. I can't decide. |
| ANA | You and Joseph must have the same brain. Can't you decide anything? |
| MADISON | Ana, please stop saying things like that. You're not helping us at all. |
| ANA | So? |
| SPENCER | Seeoowo, you always have good ideas. What do you think? |
| SEEOOWO | Well, I think we should choose drawing. That usually makes everyone feel better. |
| JOSEPH | Ana, see how Spencer told Seeoowo she has good ideas? That probably makes her feel really good. Why don't you try it? [Turns to Spencer.] **Spencer, you have good ideas, too. Which one do you think we should choose?** |

*Continued on next page*

## Skill 25

# Giving Put-Ups—Continued

**Script B**

SPENCER    I agree with Seeoowo. Let's choose a drawing!

MADISON    Ana, you're making us feel bad. Spencer and Seeoowo are encouraging us. That helps us feel good.

ANA    Oh, right. The way you think is pathetic.

CATHERINE    Putting us down doesn't help anyone, Ana. In fact, it makes us feel like giving up!

SPENCER    I learned that giving people put-ups helps everyone feel more comfortable.

MADISON    And, giving put-ups helps the group work together, and then everyone tries harder. Put-downs make us feel different and unwelcome.

SEEOOWO    If everyone used put-downs, I'd feel very uncomfortable. I wouldn't want to say anything or work together in our group.

ANA    [To the entire group] I didn't know you were so sensitive.

JOSEPH    It just makes sense, Ana. Using put-ups helps everyone know their contributions are welcome.

## Skill 26

# Participating

**Staging**

### Definition

Doing your part in a group.

### Activities/Discussions

1. Show students a picture of an ice cream sundae. Lead a discussion about what it would taste like without one of the ingredients and how all the parts work together to make the sundae complete.

2. Describe a group as being similar to an ice cream sundae: members have to do their part to be successful. Ask students to describe the main ingredients of a successful group, using these aspects as a guide:

   - Everyone takes part
   - Everyone is accountable (i.e., must account for her/his actions)
   - Everyone talks face-to-face about what works and what doesn't
   - Everyone participates in the group's decisions

3. Ask students for examples of participating in groups. List them on an overhead or on the board under four headings:

   - Taking part
   - Accounting for actions
   - Participating in group decisions
   - Talking face-to-face about what works and what doesn't

---

## Alternative Settings

☐ **Home**—Your family is sitting down for a family meeting. Describe to them what you have learned about participating so that the group is successful in reaching its goal.

☐ **School**—One member of your group often takes over and does everyone else's job. Describe what you would say to that person about participating in the group.

☐ **Community**—You and your brother have gone to the library for the weekly fun club, where you do art projects based on books. You are put into a group with four people you don't know and are given materials to make a mask that somehow depicts a character from a specific book. Show how you would do your part in the group.

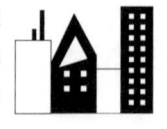

*Skill 26*

# Participating

**Number of Characters:** 5

**Character Descriptions:** Student group members:
- Logan
- Cody
- Jasmine
- Megan
- Haley

**Scene Description:** Ms. Glock's science class is studying bats. As part of their studies, each group gets to choose to do one of the following projects related to bats: a play, a poem, a short story, or a set of illustrations. The scene begins when the group begins discussing which project to choose.

## Script A

# Skill 26

# Participating

LOGAN [Looks at the other students.] **How should we start?**

CODY **I think we should each say what we want to do and then vote.**

JASMINE **I like that idea. It sounds fair to me.**

[Other students nod in agreement.]

MEGAN **I'll be glad to count the votes.** [Takes out paper and pencil.] **Who wants to do a play?**

[Logan and Haley raise their hands.]

MEGAN [Writes down their votes.] **How many want to do a poem?**

[Cody raises his hand. Megan writes it down.]

MEGAN **How many want to do a short story?**

[None of the students vote for this.]

MEGAN **How many want to do a set of illustrations?**

[Jasmine raises her hand. Megan writes it down.]

MEGAN **I'd like to do the illustrations, too.** [Adds her name to the votes and counts them.] **Two for the play, two for the illustrations, one for the poem, and none for the short story. It's a tie between the play and the illustrations. What do you want to do now?**

HALEY **The play and the illustrations got the most votes. Let's vote between those two.**

[Other students voice their agreement.]

*Continued on next page*

## Skill 26

# Participating—*Continued*

MEGAN  **OK, how many for the play?**

[Logan, Haley, and Cody raise their hands.]

MEGAN  **Looks like we do the play. Jasmine, maybe we could do some illustrations on our own time. Want to come over after school to work on it?**

JASMINE  **OK. That's a good idea.** [Turns to the other members of the group.] **What can I do to help with the play?**

CODY  **Let's see. We need to figure out what to say. I'll be happy to write everything down.**

LOGAN  **I can look up anything we need from the Internet during computer time.**

HALEY  [To Jasmine and Megan] **We'll need a bat set and bat costumes. Would you two want to work on those? It's not the same as illustrations, but it's close.**

JASMINE  **Cool! I'd like to draw the set. Megan, would you draw some costumes?**

MEGAN  **Sure. In fact, why don't we make gigantic drawings and use those instead of making an actual set and costumes? We're not going to have time, anyway.**

LOGAN  **Yeah! Haley, Cody, and I can start writing what we want to say, and you can start working on the drawings. We have 10 minutes right now.**

[Everyone agrees to this plan. Haley, Cody, and Logan move their chairs together and start talking about what to write. Jasmine and Megan get out paper and markers and start drawing their ideas.]

*Skill 26*

# Participating

**Setting B**

**Number of Characters:** 5

**Character Descriptions:** Student group members:
- Connor
- Haley
- Austin
- Brianna
- Morgan

**Props:** Backpack

**Scene Description:** The learning groups in Mr. Belofsky's social studies class are working on their entries in the school song contest. The students have been working on their songs for several days. The scene begins just after Mr. Belofsky has instructed the students to get into their groups to work on the song.

## Skill 26

# Participating

**Script B**

[Connor and Haley stand together and talk.]

CONNOR   **What did you have for lunch, Haley?**

HALEY   **Spaghetti. What did you have?**

CONNOR   **I had spaghetti, too. I'd rather have tacos, though.**

HALEY   **Me, too. I think tacos are on the menu tomorrow.**

AUSTIN   [Calls to Connor and Haley from where the group is sitting.] **Hey, Connor, Haley! Come on! We can't start without you!**

CONNOR   [Doesn't move.] **Yeah, yeah, yeah. There's plenty of time.**

HALEY   [Starts walking toward the group.] **Coming!**

BRIANNA   **Morgan, do you have our notes from this morning?**

MORGAN   **Um hm. Here, let's see what we said we were going to do. Connor and Austin were going to look up synonyms for our mascot, the wildcat. Haley was going to make up some tunes to try out. Brianna was going to write two sets of words. I guess the words for a song are called lyrics. And I agreed to keep our records because I'm not very good with music.**

HALEY   [Sits down with the group.] **Here are two ideas I had for the tune. See what you think.** [Hums two sets of tunes.]

AUSTIN   **I like both of them. It's going to be hard to decide. Connor, are you coming?**

[Connor sits down with a different group.]

BRIANNA   **I'll read these lyrics out loud so we can see which ones go with which tune.**

*Continued on next page*

*Peer Interaction Skills*

# Skill 26

# Participating—Continued

MORGAN: **Good idea. Maybe hearing the lyrics will help us decide which tune to use.**

BRIANNA: **These aren't finished, though. I still need the synonyms so I can put them in the right places.**

[Connor comes over and sits with his group.]

AUSTIN: **Connor and I found some synonyms for** *wildcats*. **Connor, where's the paper we wrote those on?**

CONNOR: [Takes everything out of his backpack but doesn't find the paper.] **I can't find it. I must've left it at home.**

BRIANNA: **Connor, we were counting on you to do your part. We can't finish the lyrics without those words.**

CONNOR: **I know. I'm sorry.**

MORGAN: **It's hard to work with you, Connor, when you don't take it seriously. You're affecting all of us.**

AUSTIN: **Yeah, Connor, we all have to do our part to be successful. We want to write a good song, but we need you to do your part.**

CONNOR: [To the entire group] **I'm really sorry. I know you're right.** [Smiles.] **But I remember the words we found yesterday:** *lynx* **and** *ocelot.*

BRIANNA: **Oh, good, I can use** *lynx* **in this lyric. It rhymes with** *thinks,* **see? Right here. Listen now and see what you think.**

## Skill 27

# Staying on Task

### Definition
Giving your full attention to the group.

### Activities/Discussions

1. Ask students for situations in which it is important to stay on task and to give their full attention. Write their examples on an overhead or on the board under the headings: *school, work, home, public situations*. Reinforce cognitive planning skills.

2. Ask students to describe various ways people pay attention. Then narrow the discussion to focus on the two types of attending required for working in a group:

   - Attending to oneself–what am I doing?
   - Attending to others–what are they doing?

3. Ask students for examples of how they show they are giving their full attention to their group. List their examples on an overhead or on the board under these headings:

   - Listening to other group members
   - Maintaining eye contact with group members and group materials
   - Staying seated with the group

---

## Alternative Settings

☐ **Home**—Your family has weekly meetings to talk about what's going on, upcoming activities, chores, allowances, and making decisions. During a meeting, your younger sister keeps kicking you under the table and trying to get your attention. Show how you would give your full attention to the group. Tell about attending to yourself.

☐ **School**—At the beginning of math class, you are thinking about going to your friend's house after school. Then your teacher tells you to get into your math groups. Show how you would stay on task and give your full attention to your math group.

☐ **Community**—You belong to a service club that meets after school. This week's meeting is being held in the cafeteria, where several other clubs are meeting at the same time. Show how you can stay on task and give full attention to the members of your club.

*Skill 27*

# Staying on Task

**Number of Characters:** 5

**Character Descriptions:** Student group members:
- Cooper
- Braden
- Ally
- Andres
- Kelli

**Props:** Clue box; can of Diet Coke®; can of regular Coke®; large basin of water; instruction sheet

**Scene Description:** Each group in Mr. Mack's class is conducting an experiment on buoyancy, or being able to float. The students have gathered the necessary materials and are following their teacher's written instructions for their experiment.

*Skill 27*

# Staying on Task

**Script A**

COOPER  [Picks up two Coke cans, one regular and one diet. Looks at other group members.] **Who's got the instructions? What are we supposed to do with these?**

BRADEN  [Reads from the instruction sheet.] **I do. "Place each of the Coke cans into the sink full of water and see which one floats."**

ALLY  **Let me see those cans.** [Cooper shows the cans to everyone in the group.] **So, one is diet and one is regular? That's the only difference?**

ANDRES  **Looks like it. This one says "diet" and this one doesn't. Drop them in the water, Cooper.**

[Cooper places the cans in the water. All the students watch as one can floats and the other one doesn't. The students in another group break out in laughter and noisy talking.]

KELLI  [Talks over the noise of the other group.] **That's weird. Which one sank?**

ALLY  [Picks up the floating can.] **This is the diet Coke. Why would the regular Coke sink?**

BRADEN  [Reads from instruction sheet.] **"To help you discover why one can sinks and one can floats, look at the list of ingredients."**

ALLI  [Reads from the ingredients on the diet Coke.] **"Carbonated water, caramel color, aspartame. . . ." What's aspartame?**

ANDRES  **It's fake sugar, I think. We learned about it in the nutrition unit.**

*Continued on next page*

*Peer Interaction Skills*

149

## Skill 27

# Staying on Task—Continued

ALLI **Oh, yeah, I remember.** [To Kelli and Braden, who are reading the ingredients on the regular Coke can] **What does it say on that can?**

KELLI **This one says, "Carbonated water, high fructose corn syrup and/or sucrose, caramel color . . ."**

COOPER [Excitedly] **That's it! See, this one** [Indicates the diet Coke.] **says "aspartame," and this one** [Indicates the regular Coke.] **says "high fructose corn syrup." Why would corn syrup make it sink?**

[Another group squeals in delight when their Coke can sinks.]

ANDRES [Talks over the other group's voices.] **I don't know! Braden, what does it say to do next?**

BRADEN [Again reads from the instruction sheet.] **"When you think you have discovered what made one can sink and one can float, look in the Clue Box on my desk for another clue."**

ALLI [Looks at each of the members of her group.] **Maybe just one of us should go get the clue. It's too noisy for all of us to go. Who wants to go?**

ANDRES **I'll go. I'll be right back!** [Goes to the Clue Box, takes out the clue for his group, and comes right back.]

KELLI **What does it say, Andres?**

ANDRES [Reads the clue aloud.] **"Corn syrup is denser than artificial sweetener."**

BRADEN **That means it's heavier, doesn't it?**

COOPER **Yeah, that's why the regular Coke sank and the diet one didn't! Cool!**

[The students continue with the experiment.]

## Skill 27

# Staying on Task

**Number of Characters:** 5

**Character Descriptions:** Student group members:
- Dominic
- Marissa
- Xavier
- Marcus
- Jocelyn

**Props:** Crayons and paper

**Scene Description:** Ms. Contreras's class is studying reptiles and amphibians. This group has been assigned to report to the class on the differences between reptiles and amphibians. For the past week and a half, the students have observed frog eggs developing into tadpoles and the tadpoles developing into frogs. The group is meeting to decide what to include in their report.

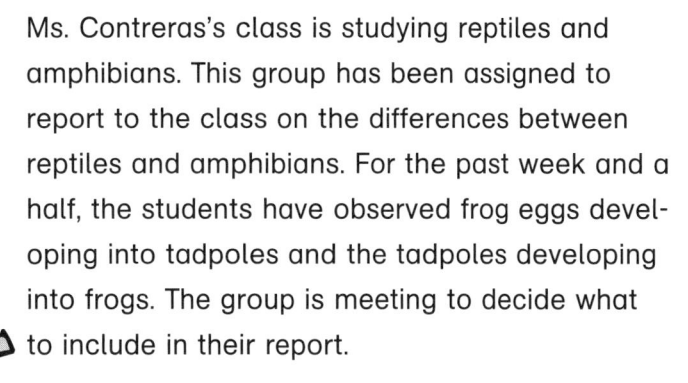

## Skill 27

# Staying on Task

DOMINIC — **Let's all say what we think should be in the report.**

MARISSA — **I'm excited about my grandmother coming to visit tonight.**

XAVIER — **I think we should do a drawing of how the eggs looked, and a drawing of how the tadpoles looked, and then a drawing showing the frogs.**

JOCELYN — **Cool! We can show the pictures when we talk about how amphibians live.**

MARCUS — **What can we say to tell how amphibians are different from reptiles?**

DOMINIC — **We can say amphibians are the only animals that live in water part of their lives and on land for another part.**

XAVIER — [Looks at Marissa.] **What do you think, Marissa.** [Marissa turns her head away and shrugs.] **We can also say that amphibians can breathe through gills or their skin. And that they can't live where it's very cold.**

JOCELYN — **And that amphibians don't shed their skin like reptiles.**

XAVIER — **Hmm. Maybe we need to do different drawings, then. Maybe we should do one of a frog and one of a snake to show how they're different.**

DOMINIC — **We could do one showing a snake shedding its skin.**

MARCUS — **That might be too hard to draw.**

*Continued on next page*

## Skill 27

# Staying on Task—Continued

**Script B**

| | |
|---|---|
| MARISSA | **I'm too excited to think about amphibians and reptiles.** |
| JOCELYN | **This is a group project, Marissa. We're trying to plan our report and to include drawings to make it more interesting.** |
| DOMINIC | **I bet you could draw it, Marissa. You're good at drawing. Besides, we need you to be part of this group. Would you try drawing it?** |
| XAVIER | **Yeah, Marissa, you're our best artist. You'll see your grandmother tonight. Could you do the drawing now?** |
| MARISSA | **Oh, OK, I'm just so excited to see her, I'm having trouble concentrating.** [Gets her crayons out.] **What color should I make the snake?** |
| MARCUS | **Make it green and blue, really colorful. And make the skin real dull, maybe coming off behind it to show it's shedding.** |
| MARISSA | [Begins drawing.] **Who's drawing the frog?** |
| DOMINIC | **I will! I love drawing frogs!** [Gets out his crayons and begins drawing.] |
| XAVIER | **OK. Jocelyn, Marcus, and I will start writing what to say.** |
| | [The students work quietly for several minutes.] |
| MARISSA | **This is fun!** [Looks up from her drawing at Xavier, Marcus, and Jocelyn.] **We could also say that amphibians lay their eggs in water, and reptiles lay theirs on land.** |
| JOCELYN | **Yeah, that's good. We'll put that in the report, too.** |

*Peer Interaction Skills*

## Skill 28

# Disagreeing Politely

**Staging**

### Definition
Telling someone you don't agree, without giving a put-down.

### Activities/Discussions

1. Ask students what they think *agree* and *disagree* mean. Write their meanings on an overhead or on the board under the two words. Emphasize the concepts of sharing (agreeing) and not sharing (disagreeing) an opinion, belief, or idea.

2. Ask students for examples of polite things people say to each other when they agree and disagree. Again, list these under the respective words.

3. Have students draw a picture of two people politely disagreeing, and two people impolitely disagreeing. Being sensitive to cultural variations, have the students describe how they decided to depict the two situations.

------

## Alternative Settings

☐ **Home**—Your sister tells you about her favorite band. Show how you would politely disagree with her without using a put-down.

☐ **School**—When you finish telling your class about your favorite book, one of your classmates tells you you're wrong. Show how you will politely disagree without using a put-down. Remember to calm down, think, then act.

☐ **Community**—You've just found another in your favorite series of comic books, and you are waiting in line to pay for it. The person behind you tells you the book you have is terrible. Show how you will politely disagree without using a put-down.

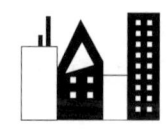

## Skill 28

# Disagreeing Politely

**Number of Characters:** 4

**Character Descriptions:** Three friends:
- Cole
- Jesse
- Paige

Narrator

**Props:** Ball

**Scene Description:** The three friends are playing with a ball in the back yard. At first, they just kick it around and chase it. The scene begins when they decide to make up some rules.

> No, thanks.

> Not today.

> I'm sorry. I can't.

## Script A

# Skill 28
# Disagreeing Politely

COLE  [Picks up the ball.] **I think we should play keep-away. I'll throw it to Paige and Jesse tries to get it.**

PAIGE  **I have a different idea. How about if we take turns kicking it and the other two try to catch it?**

JESSE  [To Paige] **Or, Cole could kick it to you, you could kick it to me, and I could kick it to Cole.**

COLE  **I don't agree. I think it's more fun to play keep-away.**

JESSE  **It's not as much fun when you're little, like Paige. It wouldn't be fair for her.**

PAIGE  **Yeah, you'll just throw the ball so high, I'll never get it.**

COLE  **Hmm. What if we get the softball and bat and one person hits it to the others?**

PAIGE  **That sounds fun. Do you know where they are, Jesse?**

JESSE  **No, but I'll look under the porch. That's where my little brother usually leaves them.**

NARRATOR  [Jesse finds the equipment. The children play for several minutes and then go inside for a snack. Jesse's mother has left them several kinds of fruit and yogurt.]

JESSE  **Oh, look! I think cantaloupe is the best fruit.**

COLE  **I like grapes the best. They're like drinking juice!**

*Continued on next page* ➤

## Skill 28

# Disagreeing Politely—Continued

PAIGE     I disagree with both of you. I think the watermelon is the best. It quenches my thirst right away!

JESSE     [Laughs.] Good thing we don't agree, isn't it? I'll eat the cantaloupe, and you two can have those other fruits!

COLE     OK, I'll take these grapes!

PAIGE     And I'll take this watermelon!

[The friends stand happily munching on their snacks.]

No, thanks.

Not today.

I'm sorry. I can't.

# Skill 28
# Disagreeing Politely

**Number of Characters:** 5

**Character Descriptions:** Student group members:
- Rina
- Nora
- Roxanne
- Isaac
- Victor

**Scene Description:** Each group in Ms. Li's class is deciding which of their units to display in the hallway outside their classroom. The scene begins when the students in the group begin talking about what they think is their best unit to display.

*No, thanks.*

*Not today.*

*I'm sorry. I can't.*

## Skill 28

# Disagreeing Politely

RINA — I think our best unit is the one on oceans. The mural is really beautiful and would look good on the wall.

NORA — No way! The mural is good, but it's not as good as the illustrations we did for the astronomy unit.

ROXANNE — You're both wrong. The best one is our solar system unit. We could put up pictures of all those planets we made. Or we could put the planet models in that case by the drinking fountain.

ISAAC — Wait a minute. You're both using put-downs instead of disagreeing politely.

NORA — What do you mean? I was just stating my opinion.

VICTOR — Nora, what you said wasn't exactly a put-down, but you could say it more politely.

NORA — Oops! I forgot we were working on disagreeing politely. Sorry, Rina.

RINA — Oh, no problem. I disagree with you about the astronomy illustrations, though. I still think we should use the oceans mural.

ROXANNE — That's dumb! Why wouldn't we want to show the planets?

ISAAC — Roxanne, we need your help to make this decision. Could you try to disagree more politely?

ROXANNE — OK, OK. I'll disagree more politely. Rina, I disagree with your idea. I think we should use the planets for our display.

*Continued on next page*

# Skill 28

# Disagreeing Politely—Continued

RINA    Maybe we should vote. Does anyone else have one you'd like to consider?

ISAAC    Yes. I disagree with all of you. I'd like to use the technology unit. For our display, we could use computer printouts to show all the different kinds of technology we studied.

VICTOR    I like that idea, too. But I also like the idea of using the oceans mural. Rina's right; it is beautiful.

RINA    We can settle the disagreement by voting. Shall we do that?

[They nod their heads in agreement and take the vote.]

*No, thanks.*

*Not today.*

*I'm sorry. I can't.*

## Skill 29

# Taking Charge of Feelings

## Definition
Knowing you have control over how to express your feelings.

## Activities/Discussions

1. Ask students how they know when they feel:

   - Happiness
   - Joy
   - Fear
   - Sadness
   - Unhappiness
   - Confidence
   - Well-being
   - Anger
   - Uncertainty

2. Explain to students that they control how they express their feelings. Brainstorm responsible and irresponsible ways to express the emotions listed above. Review posture, facial expression, volume, and other appropriate skills.

3. Have students draw a picture of themselves feeling happy and confident.

---

## Alternative Settings

☐ **Home**—Your brother borrowed one of your toys without asking. How would you feel? Show how you would responsibly express your displeasure.

☐ **School**—An older student pushes you in the hallway. How would you feel? Show how you would remind yourself that you're in charge of your actions. Remember to calm down, think, then act.

☐ **Community**—Your coach has made you sit on the bench during the last two games. Show how you could talk to her to express your feelings in a responsible way.

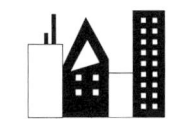

## Skill 29

# Taking Charge of Feelings

**Number of Characters:** 4

**Character Descriptions:** Zachary—a student
Alexis—a student
Nathan—a student
Ms. Potts—the drama teacher

**Scene Description:** Zachary, Alexis, and Nathan are performing in a play Ms. Potts is putting on for the community. The scene begins the afternoon the play opens. The students are talking in the drama room.

*Skill 29*

# Taking Charge of Feelings

**Script A**

| | |
|---|---|
| ZACHARY | I can't believe we're going to be on stage in just three hours. I'm so excited I can hardly stand it! |
| ALEXIS | Me too! But I'm really scared. Are either of you scared? |
| NATHAN | I am. Every time I think about going on stage for the first time tonight, my heart beats faster. |
| ZACHARY | I'm glad to know you're both scared, too. I was embarrassed to tell you I'm scared. I wonder if Ms. Potts is scared. She's done this so many times she's probably used to it. |
| ALEXIS | Ms. Potts? |
| | [Ms. Potts comes over to where the students are talking.] |
| ALEXIS | We were wondering if you're ever scared on the first night of a show. |
| NATHAN | We're all scared, but we thought you must be used to this by now. |
| MS. POTTS | Oh, no, I'm not used to it yet! [Laughs.] I'm not sure I'll ever be used to it. |
| ZACHARY | How do you know you're scared? |
| MS. POTTS | Usually, my stomach turns flip-flops. Sometimes I get short of breath. |
| NATHAN | My heart beats really fast when I think about going on stage tonight. |
| MS. POTTS | What about you, Alexis, Nathan? |

*Continued on next page*

Scripting Junior © 2004 Thinking Publications
Duplication permitted for educational use only.

## Skill 29
# Taking Charge of Feelings—Continued

**Script A**

| | |
|---|---|
| ALEXIS | **My mouth gets so dry I'm afraid it'll get stuck!** [They all laugh together.] |
| NATHAN | **Mine, too, and I'm afraid my voice won't come out.** [Giggles nervously.] |
| MS. POTTS | **Well, this all sounds pretty normal to me. All actors feel some kind of fear or nervousness when they're first learning to act. Most of them say they never get over those feelings.** |
| ZACHARY | **Do you think we'll do OK once we start?** |
| MS. POTTS | **You'll do just fine. Some nervousness is probably a good thing. It keeps you alert.** |
| ALEXIS | **Thanks, Ms. Potts, for talking to us about this. We were all a little embarrassed to tell anyone we're scared.** |
| MS. POTTS | **You're right on track, taking charge of your feelings like this. And, you've talked about them in a very honest way. You should all pat yourselves on the back for a job well done!** |
| NATHAN | **Thanks, Ms. Potts. I feel much better now. See you later!** |
| ZACHARY AND ALEXIS | **See you later!** |

*Conflict Resolution and Community Interaction Skills*

164

**Scripting Junior** © 2004 Thinking Publications
Duplication permitted for educational use only.

## Skill 29

# Taking Charge of Feelings

**Number of Characters:** 3

**Character Descriptions:** Three friends
- Kelsey
- Mason
- Jordan

**Scene Description:** The three friends are having a snack at Mason's house one day after school. All the children are sad because Mason's dog died the day before.

*Skill 29*

# Taking Charge of Feelings

**Script B**

| | |
|---|---|
| MASON | I can't believe he died. He's been sick before, but he always got well. |
| KELSEY | What happened? |
| MASON | He just stopped eating and drinking. My mom and dad took him to the vet, but there was nothing they could do. The vet said he had liver cancer. |
| JORDAN | Did you get to go see him? |
| MASON | Yes, my parents wanted me to say goodbye to him. |
| KELSEY | Wasn't that hard? Did you cry? |
| MASON | [Angrily] No! I didn't cry! What makes you think I would cry, anyway? |
| KELSEY | Mason, don't get mad! I was just trying to find out how you felt. |
| MASON | I didn't cry! |
| JORDAN | I feel like crying. I miss him already. He always used to be here, wagging his tail and licking me. He was so sweet. |
| KELSEY | I know. I was never afraid of him because he was such a cutie. |
| MASON | [Still angry] You don't know how it feels! |
| KELSEY | No, we don't. And we won't know until you tell us, either. If you just stay mad, we'll never know. And you'll just keep feeling bad. |

*Continued on next page*

## Skill 29
# Taking Charge of Feelings—Continued

MASON  [Surprised] **What do you mean?**

JORDAN  **She's talking about taking charge of your feelings, Mason. Have you stopped to think how you feel? Remember when we worked on this in class?**

KELSEY  **Remember how we learned to take deep breaths and count to 10? And then we paid attention to how our bodies felt?**

MASON  **Yeah.**

KELSEY  **What if you do that now?**

[Mason takes some deep breaths and counts to 10. A few moments pass.]

MASON  **I think I feel very sad.**

JORDAN  **Yeah, me too.**

KELSEY  **I'm glad to know he didn't suffer, though.**

MASON  **Yeah, the vet said he didn't feel any pain at all, so that's a good thing.**

JORDAN  **Do you think you'll ever get another dog?**

MASON  **I don't know. Right now I can't even think about it. Maybe when I stop feeling so sad.**

## Skill 30

# Being Assertive

### Definition
Standing up for yourself in a confident and respectful way.

### Activities/Discussions

1. Discuss with students how they feel when someone does and does not respect their rights, feelings, or beliefs. Discuss the difference between *assertive* and *aggressive* by defining each. *Assertive* means standing up for our beliefs, feelings, or rights. *Aggressive* means attacking or disregarding others' beliefs, feelings, or rights.

2. Ask students for examples of how people can assert their rights, feelings, or beliefs confidently and respectfully. List them on an overhead or on the board under these headings:

   - Words
   - Actions
   - Tone of voice
   - Body talk
   - Facial expressions

   Emphasize the importance of cognitive planning strategies.

3. Have students draw a picture of how they feel when they stand up for their rights, beliefs, or feelings.

------

## Alternative Settings

☐ **Home**—You are listening to music in your room when your brother arrives home from school. He comes into your room and tells you the band you're listening to is not as good as his favorite band. Show how you would stand up for your belief that your favorite band is worth listening to.

☐ **School**—A member of your group tells you that you can't be the team leader because you're not organized well enough. Show how you would respond assertively.

☐ **Community**—You and some friends are standing in line to buy tickets at the movie theater. Some other kids you know cut in line in front of you. Demonstrate an assertive response.

## Skill 30

# Being Assertive

**Number of Characters:** 4

**Character Descriptions:** Garrett–a student
Lucas–a student
Melanie–a student
Jackson–a student

**Scene Description:** On the way home from school, Garrett and Lucas are stopped by some older kids, Melanie and Jackson, who want them to help tear down the basketball net on the playground.

## Script A

# Skill 30

# Being Assertive

| MELANIE | Hey, come help us tear down the basketball net! Hold the fence open so we can climb through. |
|---|---|
| JACKSON | Yeah, you can help us climb the pole to get the net too. C'mon! |
| GARRETT | I'm not going to help you do that! I don't do things like that. Besides, it's school property. |
| MELANIE | So? Who cares? |
| LUCAS | I care! I'm not going to help you! |
| JACKSON | Ah, you're just scared, that's all. Nobody's going to see us. C'mon! |
| LUCAS | No, I'm not doing it. Leave us alone! |
| GARRETT | Yeah, leave us alone! We're not helping you. |
| MELANIE | You're stupid! C'mon, Jackson, let's leave these jerks here. They're too dumb to help, anyway. |
| GARRETT | We're not stupid, we're not jerks, and we're not dumb. We don't like being called names. |
| LUCAS | Leave us alone! |

[Melanie and Jackson run toward the basketball court.]

| GARRETT | I don't like being called names, do you? |
|---|---|
| LUCAS | No, and I'm not going to destroy school property, either. Let's get out of here. |

**Be Assertive!**

## Skill 30

# Being Assertive

**Number of Characters:** 4

**Character Descriptions:** Nathaniel and Jade—twins
Ms. Graves—the twins' mother
Mr. Graves—the twins' father

**Scene Description:** Nathaniel and Jade's parents have just given them their household job lists for the week.

## Script B

# Skill 30

# Being Assertive

[Nathaniel and Jade look at each other. Nathaniel raises his eyebrows. Jade looks down.]

**NATHANIEL** **You always give Jade the easiest jobs! Why do I always have to take out the trash? She never has to!**

**JADE** **I always have to take out the kitty litter! Every day, too! That's not so easy!**

**NATHANIEL** **Oh, right, like kitty litter is such a hard job.**

**JADE** **Well, it is! It's harder than taking out the trash once a week.**

**MR. GRAVES** **Whoa! What's happening here?**

**JADE** [Angrily] **He's saying my job is easier than his!**

**NATHANIEL** **Well, it is!**

**MS. GRAVES** **Wait a minute. I seem to remember you're both learning about being assertive in your class. Is that right?**

**JADE** **Yes.**

**MS. GRAVES** **Nathaniel, tell me what you learned about being assertive.**

**NATHANIEL** **We learned how to speak up for ourselves in a confident and respectful way.**

**MR. GRAVES** **Is that what you did just now?**

**NATHANIEL** **Well. . . . No.**

**MR. GRAVES** **Is that what you did, Jade?**

*Continued on next page*

## Skill 30

# Being Assertive—Continued

| | |
|---|---|
| JADE | **I guess not.** |
| MS. GRAVES | **Let's start over, then. Nathaniel, you spoke first, so you start. How can you speak up for yourself about the job list?** |
| NATHANIEL | [Thinks for a moment.] **Mom, Dad, I think the jobs you give me are harder than the ones you give Jade. I don't think it's fair.** |
| MR. GRAVES | **Jade, what do you have to say to that?** |
| JADE | [Sits straight and looks at parents.] **I'd like to switch jobs with Nathaniel sometimes. That way I wouldn't get bored doing the same thing all the time.** |
| MS. GRAVES | [To Mr. Graves] **Those sound like reasonable requests to me. What do you think?** |
| MR. GRAVES | **I agree. You both have a good point.** [To Nathaniel] **I didn't realize you were unhappy, and** [To Jade] **I didn't realize you wanted a change. Let's re-do this list so you both feel better about it.** |
| MS. GRAVES | **I appreciate you both using what you know about assertiveness to change how you talked about this. You're both learning the right way to speak up for yourselves!** |

*Skill 31*

# Being Responsible

## Definition
Choosing to do what is right.

## Activities/Discussions

1. Ask students for examples of their responsibilities and list them under these headings:
   - Home
   - School
   - Community

2. Discuss with students how the examples they provided reflect choices to do what is right. Emphasize cognitive planning skills. Give them some rules of thumb for acting responsibly. For instance, have them ask themselves, "Would I like to go home and tell my parents what I did?"

3. Discuss the difference between being responsible (choosing to do what is right) and being assertive (standing up for yourself in a confident and respectful way).

------

## Alternative Settings

☐ **Home**—You accidentally delete an important file on your sister's computer. Show what you can do and say to be responsible. Remember to calm down, think, then act.

☐ **School**—Your science teacher had agreed to stay after school to help you with an assignment. That day, your friends ask you to go with them to play ball in the park. Show how you will be responsible.

☐ **Community**—Several sheets of newspaper are blowing across your elderly neighbor's yard. Show what you would do to be responsible.

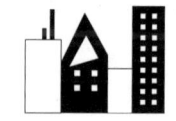

## Skill 31

# Being Responsible

**Number of Characters:** 6

**Character Descriptions:** Ms. Castenada, School Principal
Antonio–a student
Colin–a student
Evan–a student
Zoe–a student
Ms. Martinelli–Zoe's mother

**Props:** Chairs arranged like auditorium seats; microphone

**Scene Description:** Antonio, Colin, Evan, and Zoe are sitting together during a school assembly. The scene begins just after they have taken their chairs.

# Skill 31

# Being Responsible

**Script A**

| | |
|---|---|
| ANTONIO | Does anyone know what this assembly is about? |
| COLIN | Mr. Fraser said it was about school safety. He said some police officers are going to talk to us. |
| ZOE | Yeah, my mom's coming. She told me this morning she'd be here for the assembly. |
| ANTONIO | Why is your mom coming? |
| ZOE | She's a police officer. |
| EVAN | Cool! I didn't know your mom was a police officer! |
| ANTONIO | How long has she been a police officer? |
| ZOE | Eleven years. |
| COLIN | That's a long time. Does she like it? |
| ZOE | Yeah. But she says she worries about my brother and me, you know, if something would happen to her. |
| | [The school principal walks to the microphone and asks the students for quiet.] |
| EVAN | Shhh. Ms. Castenada is telling us to be quiet. |
| ZOE | [Whispers.] OK. |
| ANTONIO | [Whispers to Zoe.] Can I meet your mom? |
| ZOE | [Whispers to Antonio.] Shhh. We can talk after, OK? |
| | [Antonio nods in agreement. They turn their attention to the stage.] |
| | [After the assembly, Zoe takes Antonio, Colin, and Evan over to her mother.] |

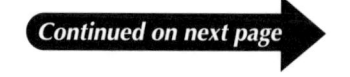

*Continued on next page*

## Skill 31

# Being Responsible—Continued

ZOE — Hi, Mom! You know Colin and Evan, and this is Antonio. He wanted to meet you.

MS. MARTINELLI — Hello, Zoe. Hi, Colin. Hi, Evan. How do you do, Antonio?

ANTONIO — Hello.

MS. MARTINELLI — I noticed that you all stopped talking as soon as Ms. Castenada asked for quiet. Zoe has told me you're learning about acting responsibly. It sure showed today! Nice job, kids! And Zoe, you did a nice job introducing your friends to me. Thanks, Zoe.

## Skill 31

# Being Responsible

**Number of Characters:** 5

**Character Descriptions:** Four children:
- Carson
- Claire
- Mariah
- Rafe–Carson's older brother

Narrator

**Scene Description:** Carson, Claire, and Mariah are riding their bikes in a crowded park. Rafe is talking to some friends by the drinking fountains.

## Skill 31

# Being Responsible

| | |
|---|---|
| CARSON | **C'mon, you guys! Let's ride to those trees!** [Points to some trees just beyond the swings.] |
| CLAIRE | **Bet I can beat you over there!** |
| CARSON | **Oh, no, you can't! C'mon Mariah, let's go! We can beat her!** |
| NARRATOR | [The three start through the swing area but have to turn sharply to avoid running into children on the swings. They stop at the trees.] |
| MARIAH | **That girl should look out! I almost hit her! We could have gotten hurt.** |
| CLAIRE | **Yeah, they need to pay attention to what they're doing.** |
| CARSON | **Let's go get a drink. I'm thirsty.** |
| NARRATOR | [The three ride their bikes to the drinking fountains, dodging several people along the way. They slide to a stop near Rafe.] |
| CARSON | **Hi, Rafe!** |
| RAFE | **Hi, Carson. Hi, Mariah. Hi, Claire. Do you guys know what you're doing?** |
| CARSON | **What do you mean? We're getting a drink of water.** |
| RAFE | **No, I mean do you know what you're doing on your bikes?** |
| CLAIRE | **We're having so much fun! We're riding all over the place.** |

*Continued on next page* →

## Skill 31

# Being Responsible—Continued

| | |
|---|---|
| RAFE | That's what I mean. Have you noticed any other people in this park? |
| MARIAH | [Looks around.] There are a lot of people here. |
| RAFE | Yes, and do you think it's a good idea to be riding your bikes so fast when there are this many people around? Do you think it's responsible? |
| MARIAH | Oh, I see what you mean. We didn't think about that. |
| CLAIRE | No, we didn't. We were so excited, we forgot. |
| RAFE | No wonder that girl was upset, Mariah. What can you do to show some responsibility here? |
| MARIAH | You're right. I should go over there and apologize to her. [Looks at Carson and Claire.] Will you go with me? |
| CARSON | Yeah, we should all go. Claire? You coming? |
| CLAIRE | Yes, wait for me! |

## Skill 32

# Taking Charge of Anger

## Definition

Knowing you have control over how to deal with your anger.

## Activities/Discussions

1. Ask students to describe what happens to their bodies when they feel angry. Have them mime what it looks like. List their descriptions on an overhead or on the board, using these categories:

   - My face…
   - My eyes…
   - My jaw…
   - My heart…
   - My breathing…
   - My fists…
   - My stomach…
   - My whole body…

2. Ask students what they think anger does to their health before they learn to take charge of it, emphasizing these health issues related to anger:

   - Heart attacks
   - Headaches
   - Depression
   - Family fights
   - Poor self-esteem
   - Alcohol and drug abuse

3. Ask students to give examples of how they have successfully taken charge of their anger. List their examples on on overhead or on the board. Reinforce their use of cognitive planning skills.

---

## Alternative Settings

☐ **Home**—Your brother punches you in the arm as he walks past you into the kitchen. You feel angry. Calm down. Think. Then show how you can take charge of your anger.

☐ **School**—A classmate uses your marking pens and forgets to put the caps back on. When you take them out of the bag, they leak all over. Think about "Being a Friend" (Skill 28) and "Building a Positive Reputation" (Skill 22). Demonstrate how you would take control of your anger.

☐ **Community**—You and some friends are walking home from school. Two neighbor kids start teasing you and using put-downs. Think about "Dealing with Teasing" (Skill 23), "Disagreeing Politely" (Skill 28), and "Taking Charge of Feelings" (Skill 29). Show how you would take charge of your anger.

## Skill 32

# Taking Charge of Anger

**Number of Characters:** 4

**Character Descriptions:** Students in Literature Group:
- Marshall
- Uri
- Danae
- Halle

Narrator (Optional)

**Props:** Concept map

**Scene Description:** Marshall, Uri, Danae, and Halle are in their literature group, starting their hero report from the book they have read, *Wilma Unlimited: How Wilma Rudolph Became the World's Fastest Woman\**. Marshall is recorder for the day.

\**Wilma Unlimited: How Wilma Rudolph Became the World's Fastest Woman.* (2000) by K. Krall and D. Diraz (illustrator). New York: Harcourt.

## Skill 32

# Taking Charge of Anger

*Script A*

MARSHALL — Here's the concept map we're supposed to follow.

URI — Let's see it. What are we supposed to include in our report?

[Everyone looks at the concept map.]

DANAE — First, we're supposed to describe what she did. Then we're supposed to tell why she is a hero.

MARSHALL — OK, let's start with what she did. The main thing is that she was a famous track and field star. She was the first American woman to win three gold medals in one Olympics.

[Halle tries to say something, but Uri interrupts her.]

URI — She had lots of health problems as a child like polio, pneumonia, and scarlet fever.

DANAE — So, she had a bad leg, and some people said she'd never walk again.

[Halle ties to speak again. This time Marshall talks at the same time.]

MARSHALL — Yeah, she wore a leg brace until she was 11! But her family was very loving and helped her.

[Again, Halle tries to say something. Uri interrupts her again. Halle begins to get angry.]

URI — They gave her physical therapy themselves, four times a day!

[Halle realizes she's angry now. She decides to use a strategy she's learned in school to take charge of her anger. She raises her hand, and everyone looks at her.]

*Continued on next page*

## Skill 32

# Taking Charge of Anger—Continued

**Script A**

HALLE: I'm feeling angry that you're interrupting me, Uri. And, Marshall, I'm angry that you won't stop talking when I try to say something. I'd really appreciate a chance to talk!

DANAE: She's right, you guys. We need to be more respectful of each other and listen.

MARSHALL: You're right, Halle. I'm sorry for talking when you started talking. I hope you won't stay angry with me.

URI: Me, too, Halle! I have this bad habit of interrupting people. Thanks for telling me it makes you angry. It'll help me remember to stop and listen before I barge into a conversation.

HALLE: Thank you! What I wanted to say was that Wilma Rudolph was not only the first American woman to win three gold medals in one Olympics. She was the first African-American woman to do it. That was not easy then.

DANAE: What year was that, again?

HALLE: That was in 1960.

URI: And after the Olympics, her hometown gave her a hero's parade. It was the first racially integrated parade in that town.

MARSHALL: Wait a minute! Let me write all this down in the right spot. Should we put this down for what she did, or for why she's a hero?

[The students continue their discussion.]

## *Skill 32*

# Taking Charge of Anger

**Setting B**

**Number of Characters:** 5

**Character Descriptions:** Student group members:
- Shaw
- Reid
- Alandra
- Carina

Narrator

**Props:** Poster; markers; paint; brushes

**Scene Description:** During art class, the students are working on their poster for the upcoming art fair.

*Skill 32*

# Taking Charge of Anger

**Script B**

| | |
|---|---|
| SHAW | I hope we finish this before the end of class. I don't think we'll have any more time to work on it before Friday. |
| CARINA | I'll be sorry to finish it, though. I'm really having fun! |
| ALANDRA | Me, too. I wish we could do this every week. |
| NARRATOR | [Reid gets up to go to the sink. As he walks past Carina, he jostles her arm, and she spills paint on the poster.] |
| CARINA | [Angrily] Oh, good job, Reid! Now you've totally wrecked our poster. You're such a jerk, you know it? |
| REID | Well, gosh, Carina, I was just walking past you. I didn't mean to bump your elbow. I didn't do it on purpose, you know. |
| ALANDRA | I'm afraid our poster is ruined! |
| CARINA | [Still angry] Guess whose fault that is? Reid, I can't believe you did this! |
| SHAW | Let's all just calm down a minute and think about what we can do about this. |
| | [They look at the poster. Carina is breathing fast, and she is scowling.] |
| SHAW | Why don't we just pretend we wanted it to look like this? |
| CARINA | I don't think so, Shaw! It's ruined! Look at it! |
| ALANDRA | Shaw may be right, Carina. You need to take a few deep breaths and cool off. Or why don't you walk around a little bit to calm down? |

*Continued on next page*

*Skill 32*

# Taking Charge of Anger—*Continued*

**Script B**

CARINA    [Less angry now] **Yeah, I guess you're right. Right now I feel like hitting Reid!**

REID    **Yeah, maybe you should walk around a little bit. Get a drink of water.**

NARRATOR    [Carina takes a few deep breaths, gets a drink of water, and returns to the group.]

ALANDRA    **Feel better?**

CARINA    **Yes. I have to work on taking charge of my anger. I feel awful when I let it get in my way.** [To Reid] **I'm sorry I blew up at you, Reid. I know you didn't do it on purpose.**

REID    **Yeah, I feel terrible that I bumped your arm.** [To everyone] **Do you think we can save the poster?**

[The students discuss how to save the poster.]

*Skill 33*

# Resisting Peer Pressure

## Definition
Knowing you have control over how to express your feelings.

## Activities/Discussions

1. Ask students if they know what *peer pressure* means. Lead them to understand it means someone, who is about their age, asking or expecting them to do something that they might not want to do.

2. Ask students for examples of peer pressure. List them on an overhead or on the board under these headings:

   - Positive peer pressure (doesn't necessarily need resistance)
   - Negative peer pressure (requires resistance)

3. Discuss with students ways of going against their peers to do what is right. Have them demonstrate how they could:

   - Say, "No"
   - Give a reason why you won't do something
   - Respond with humor
   - Leave or walk away
   - Get help from a friend or adult

   Reinforce any examples of cognitive planning skills.

## Alternative Settings

☐ **Home**—Your parents have limited your sister's computer time to 30 minutes each night. She wants you to let her use your computer while your parents are gone. She tells you they'll never find out. Think about "Disagreeing Politely" (Skill 28) and "Being Assertive" (Skill 30). Demonstrate how you would resist her peer pressure.

☐ **School**—One of your group members wants to use a book report from the Internet instead of writing your own. Think about "Being Responsible" (Skill 31) and "Building a Positive Reputation" (Skill 22). Demonstrate how you would resist peer pressure.

☐ **Community**—One of your friends wants you to steal a candy bar while he talks to the store clerk. Demonstrate how you would resist peer pressure.

## Skill 33

# Resisting Peer Pressure

**Setting A**

**Number of Characters:** 3

**Character Descriptions:** Larken
Bekah
Joaquim

**Scene Description:** Larken, Bekah, and Joaquim are watching movies at Larken's house. The scene begins when Larken's parents go to the next-door neighbors' house to play cards.

"Come on, we won't get caught!"

*Conflict Resolution and Community Interaction Skills*

**Script A**

―― *Skill 33* ――

# Resisting Peer Pressure

LARKEN — [Waits until her parents have closed the door.] **You want to watch the South Park movie? I know where my parents keep it.**

BEKAH — **You mean the movie and not the TV show, right?**

LARKEN — **Yeah, the movie. It's supposed to be really funny.**

JOAQUIM — **But isn't it an adult movie?**

LARKEN — **Yeah, but they'll never know. They won't be back for a couple of hours.**

BEKAH — **I don't know. . . . My parents told me I couldn't see it because it's rated R.**

LARKEN — **So what? My parents let me watch R-rated movies all the time.**

JOQUAIM — **Not mine. I don't think it's a good idea, and I'm not watching it.**

LARKEN — **Oh, come on, Joquaim. Don't be a wimp!**

JOQUAIM — **You can call me a wimp if you want, but I'm still not watching it.**

LARKEN — [In a strong, pushy way] **You'll watch it, won't you, Bekah?**

BEKAH — **No. I agree with Joquaim. It's not a good idea, and I don't even want to see it. It's too weird for me. Plus, I'm not ready for R-rated movies yet.**

*Continued on next page* ➜

# Skill 33

# Resisting Peer Pressure—*Continued*

Script A

LARKEN   **You two are chicken! I'm watching it anyway!** [Puts the movie in the player.]

JOQUAIM   **I'm leaving, then. Bekah, let's go call my mom. She'll come get us.**

BEKAH   **Yeah, let's go call her.**

LARKEN   **Oh, all right! You two are such babies!** [Puts the original movie back in the player.]

JOQUAIM   **You're so lucky, Larken. You've got so many good movies to watch!**

Setting B

# Skill 33

# Resisting Peer Pressure

**Number of Characters:** 9

**Character Descriptions:** Darsha
Teal
Ellery
A security officer
Store manager
Three younger children
Narrator

**Scene Description:** Darsha, Teal, and Ellery are at the mall, sitting on a bench watching people go past.

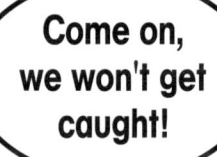

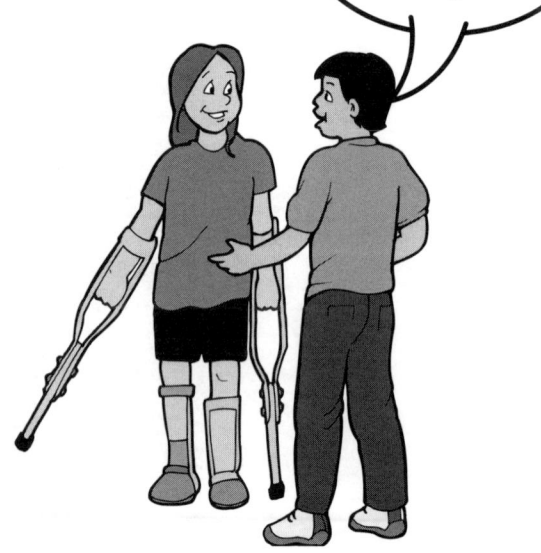

*Come on, we won't get caught!*

*Skill 33*

# Resisting Peer Pressure

**Script B**

| | |
|---|---|
| DARSHA | [Points to a store.] **Look at those kids over there.** |
| TEAL | **Look at what they're wearing. They're so pathetic.** |
| ELLERY | **They probably don't know any better. They look really young.** |
| DARSHA | **Yeah! Let's go take their money away from them!** |
| TEAL | [Hesitatingly] **I don't know.** |
| ELLERY | **It'll be easy, Teal! They'll just hand it to us, you'll see! C'mon!** |
| DARSHA | **Yeah, Teal, don't be a chicken. They'll be so scared, they'll never tell. Besides, what do we care?** |
| ELLERY | **C'mon, Teal!** |
| NARRATOR | [Ellery grabs Teal's arm and pulls her with him. They approach the younger kids.] |
| DARSHA | **Give us your money, or we'll beat you up.** |
| NARRATOR | [Two of the girls scream and run into the store.] |
| ELLERY | **Let's get out of here!** |
| NARRATOR | [Ellery and Darsha start to run. A security officer grabs Teal's arm and shouts after the other two.] |
| SECURITY OFFICER | **Stop!** |
| NARRATOR | [Ellery and Darsha keep running. The store manager walks out with the three younger children.] |
| SECURITY OFFICER | **What's going on here?** |
| STORE MANAGER | **These girls tell me this girl and her friends tried to take their money away from them.** |

*Continued on next page*

*Conflict Resolution and Community Interaction Skills*

# Skill 33

# Resisting Peer Pressure—*Continued*

| | |
|---|---|
| SECURITY OFFICER | **Is that right?** |
| TEAL | [Nods in agreement.] **I didn't want to do it.** [To the younger kids] **I'm really sorry. I know it's wrong.** [To the adults] **I felt like I couldn't say, "No" to their pressure. If I didn't go along with them, they'd tell everyone I'm a chicken.** |
| STORE MANAGER | **Sometimes it's really hard to resist peer pressure.** |
| SECURITY OFFICER | **Are you sure you want to be friends with kids like that? They'll get you into trouble, you know.** |
| TEAL | **I know. I'm not very good at standing up to peer pressure.** [Sees her parents approaching.] **Here come my mom and dad. What are you going to tell them?** |
| SECURITY OFFICER | **Let's tell them what happened and see what they say.** |
| TEAL | **OK. I know they won't like it.** |

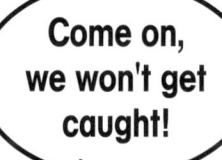

*Come on, we won't get caught!*

# Skill 34

# Settling Conflicts

## Definition
Finding a way to work out disagreements so that everyone involved feels OK.

## Activities/Discussions

1. Ask students for examples of conflicts or disagreements. List them on an overhead or on the board under the headings:

   - Very serious
   - Moderately serious
   - Mildly serious

2. Have students brainstorm ways of settling the three degrees of conflict represented in the headings above. For instance:

   - Very serious: the people involved get help from people involved in the conflict and agree to follow their recommendations (Have students generate a list of people they can trust to help.)
   - Moderately serious: the people involved cooperate and compromise on a solution
   - Mildly serious: the people involved quickly agree on a solution

3. Ask students what they think it means to "agree to disagree," and have them describe examples from their experiences that illustrate agreeing to disagree. Discuss with the students situations in which this strategy may be the best one to use.

---

## Alternative Settings

☐ **Home**—You and your parents are shopping for some new school clothes for you. You want some jeans that everyone is wearing, but your parents think they're inappropriate for you. Show how you could work out your disagreement. What should you remember?

☐ **School**—You're in line at the drinking fountain. A student cuts in front of you. You object, but then the other student calls you a name and pushes you. Show what you would do to work out the disagreement.

☐ **Community**—You and your friends disagree about which movie you are going to see. Show how you would settle the disagreement.

## Skill 34

# Settling Conflicts

**Number of Characters:** 5

**Character Descriptions:** Jesmine
Lael
Ms. Dakin–Jesmine and Lael's mother
Mr. Dakin–Jesmine and Lael's father
Narrator

**Props:** Chairs set up like a van

**Scene Description:** Starting out on a driving trip, Jesmine and Lael disagree over who gets to ride in the best seat.

## Skill 34

# Settling Conflicts

NARRATOR [Mr. and Mrs. Dakin are loading the cooler into the van. Jesmine and Lael are loading their bags.]

JESMINE [To Lael] **It's my turn to ride in the way back.**

LAEL **No, it isn't. You rode back there last time, remember? When we went to the music festival?**

JESMINE **I don't think so. I remember riding behind Mom and Dad.**

LAEL **That was the time before, when we went to Aunt Matty's for the weekend.**

JESMINE **Hmmm. Obviously, we disagree. Let's figure out a compromise. Want to play "Rock, Paper, Scissors" to decide who gets the way back?**

LAEL **That's a good idea. Or we could flip a coin. Either one would be fair.**

JESMINE **Which would you rather do?**

LAEL **You always win at "Rock, Paper, Scissors." Let's flip a coin.**

JESMINE [Laughs.] **You're right, I have been winning at "Rock, Paper, Scissors." Let's flip a coin, then. Dad, do you have a quarter?**

MR. DAKIN [Digs in his pants pocket.] **No, all I have is two dimes.**

LAEL **Those are too small. They don't flip very well. Mom, do you have a quarter?**

MS. DAKIN **Here's one.** [Hands a quarter to Lael.]

*Continued on next page*

## Skill 34

# Settling Conflicts—Continued

JESMINE    **OK, you flip and I call heads or tails, OK?**

LAEL    **OK. What do you call?**

JESMINE    **Heads.**

LAEL    [Flips the quarter, which comes up tails.] **I can't believe it! This is the first time I've won for a long time! I'll ride back here until lunch. Then you can have it until we stop. Is that fair?**

JESMINE    **Yes, that's definitely fair. Let's go!** [They climb into the van.]

## Skill 34

# Settling Conflicts

**Number of Characters:** 2

**Character Descriptions:** Von—Natalie's brother
Natalie—Von's sister

**Scene Description:** Von and Natalie are planning the special breakfast they are going to make for their mother on her birthday.

## Skill 34

# Settling Conflicts

Von    **Let's make her scrambled eggs. She likes those, especially if we put some peppers in them.**

Natalie    **She likes pancakes better. Let's make those for her. We could ask Dad to get some blueberries for us to mix into the batter.**

Von    **That's a dumb idea! I don't like pancakes. Besides, you don't even know how to make them!**

Natalie    **I thought this was supposed to be something Mom likes, not you. And, I made pancakes over at Shavon's house. It was easy; you just follow the recipe.**

Von    **Mom likes scrambled eggs better than pancakes. We could get some of that olive bread she likes for toast.**

Natalie    **No way she likes eggs better than pancakes! I've heard her say she likes pancakes better a million times!**

Von    [Angrily] **I don't think so! She always says how much she likes scrambled eggs.**

Natalie    **You don't have to get mad, Von. This is supposed to be something special for Mom. Can't you give in just once?**

Von    **That's just it, Natalie. You always want me to give in. You're never willing to compromise or figure out how to solve a disagreement.**

Natalie    [Surprised] **What do you mean?**

*Continued on next page*

# Skill 34

## Settling Conflicts—Continued

VON — I mean I have a hard time planning things with you because you usually want your way. I'd like to compromise so we both get what we want.

NATALIE — What do you suggest?

VON — One thing we could do is to flip a coin. Another thing would be to have eggs and pancakes. That way we'd both get to cook what we want.

NATALIE — Well, that might work. Won't that be too much food, though?

VON — No. Dad's always a big eater. You and I are, too. Don't worry, it won't go to waste.

NATALIE — [Grudgingly] OK, I guess I'm willing to try it. I don't like it, though. I'd rather have pancakes with blueberries.

VON — I'm going to have some of both!

# Skill 35

# Making an Apology

## Definition
Choosing words and actions that show you are sorry when you've done something.

## Activities/Discussions

1. Ask students for examples from their experiences or from current events in which an apology would make a difference in the outcome.

2. Ask students for examples of ways to express an apology. List them on an overhead or on the board, using these two headings:
   - Words
   - Actions

3. Discuss reasons why an apology might be rejected. Brainstorm strategies to use if that happens. Discuss ways to accept an apology.

------

## Alternative Settings

☐ **Home**—You scratch your father's favorite music CD. Show how you would apologize to him.

☐ **School**—You forget to bring your group the art materials you promised to bring for the science report the group is preparing. Demonstrate how you would apologize to the other group members.

☐ **Community**—At the park, you tell some younger children they can't play with you on the climbing bars. Show how you would apologize to them.

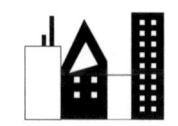

## Skill 35

# Making an Apology

**Number of Characters:** 3

**Character Descriptions:** Tatum—a student
Aunt Fran—Tatum's Aunt
Narrator

**Scene Description:** Aunt Fran told Tatum she would help her with her math homework after school. They have agreed to meet at 4:00. The scene begins with Aunt Fran waiting for Tatum.

Script A

# Skill 35

# Making an Apology

| | |
|---|---|
| NARRATOR | [Aunt Fran looks at the clock, which reads 4:15.] |
| AUNT FRAN | **I wonder where she is?** |
| NARRATOR | [Aunt Fran gets up to look out the window. At 4:25 she walks outside to look down the street. She sees Tatum running toward the house.] |
| AUNT FRAN | **Tatum! Are you OK? I've been worried that something happened to you.** |
| TATUM | [Out of breath] **Oh, Aunt Fran! I forgot you were going to help me today. I'm so sorry! We stopped for a snack, and then I remembered you were coming over.** |
| AUNT FRAN | **I'm just relieved you're alright. I couldn't imagine why you were so late.** |
| TATUM | **I apologize for making you worry. Is there something I can do to make you feel better?** |
| AUNT FRAN | **You could start by writing down your plans. Do you have a date book?** |
| TATUM | **No, but that would be a good idea. Then I could just look at it to remind myself about important plans.** |
| AUNT FRAN | **We could make you a temporary one until you can find one you like.** |
| TATUM | **OK, I'll get some paper and a pen. Will you help me organize it?** |
| AUNT FRAN | [Laughs.] **Sure, though your dad thinks I'm pretty disorganized. We'll surprise him, won't we?** |

*Continued on next page*

# Skill 35

# Making an Apology—Continued

NARRATOR [They make a one-page organizer for the current week.]

TATUM **This will work great. Where should I keep it so I don't lose it?**

AUNT FRAN **Do you have one of those plastic sleeves you can put it in? Then you can keep it in your homework notebook.**

NARRATOR [Tatum puts her homework into a plastic sleeve she has in her notebook.]

TATUM **There, this will really help me. Thanks, Aunt Fran. I'm sorry again for being late and making you worry. I won't do it again, I promise!**

AUNT FRAN **Apology accepted. Now shall we tackle that math homework?**

# Skill 35

# Making an Apology

**Number of Characters:** 3

**Character Descriptions:** Tecia–a student
Brie–a student
Fisher–a student

**Scene Description:** Tecia, Brie, and Fisher are eating lunch together. Brie playfully shakes her grape juice bottle toward Fisher. The top comes off, and grape juice spills on Fisher's clothing.

## Skill 35

# Making an Apology

TECIA     Uh, oh, that stuff doesn't come out.

FISHER     Geez, Brie, look at this mess! Now what am I going to do? My mom is going to kill me.

BRIE     I didn't do anything! The top was loose. It wasn't my fault!

FISHER     How did the top get loose? You're the only one who touched it.

TECIA     He's right, Brie. Nobody else touched your grape juice. It didn't come off by itself.

BRIE     [Angrily] No way! I'm telling you, it's not my fault!

FISHER     It's not my fault, either. My mom is never going to believe me.

BRIE     Stop blaming me! You're acting like I did it on purpose.

TECIA     He's not saying you did it on purpose, Brie. He's just upset that his clothes are probably ruined and that his mom is going to be mad at him. How would you feel if you were in his shoes?

BRIE     [Still angry] I can't believe you're taking his side.

TECIA     I'm not taking his side, Brie. I just think you should apologize to him.

BRIE     Why should I apologize? It wasn't my fault.

*Continued on next page* ➡

# Skill 35

# Making an Apology

TECIA   That doesn't really matter. The fact is that it's your grape juice that's all over his clothes. You could at least apologize to him for that.

FISHER  Yeah, Brie, you could at least apologize.

BRIE    You guys are too weird. I'm leaving. [Takes her tray and leaves the table.]

BRIE    She sure doesn't know how to be friends, does she?

FISHER  No! I don't really care whose fault it was; I just can't believe she wouldn't even apologize. Oh well. I hope my mom isn't too mad.

## Skill 36

# Responding to Criticism

## Definition
Knowing how to respond when someone suggests improvement or change in a respectful way.

## Activities/Discussions

1. Ask students what they think *criticize* means. List their responses on an overhead or on the board under these heading:

   - Positive (helpful) criticism
   - Negative (hurtful) criticism

2. Discuss with students possible strategies for responding to helpful and hurtful criticism, listing them on an overhead or on the board under those two headings. Review concepts from "Dealing with Teasing" (Skill 23), "Disagreeing Politely" (Skill 28), and "Being Assertive" (Skill 30).

3. Have students draw a picture of how they feel when they've accepted positive criticism.

------------------------------------------------------------------------

## Alternative Settings

- **Home**—Your father is giving you some helpful criticism on how you could better organize yourself for homework. Show what you could say and do to show you accept his suggestions.

- **School**—One of your classmates gives you some hurtful criticism about your art poster. Show what you could say and do to respond to her criticism. What should you remember?

- **Community**—During your visit to the neighborhood assisted-living center, one of the residents tells you how she thinks you could speak more clearly. Show what you could do and say to show you accept her suggestions.

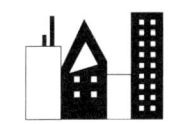

## Skill 36

# Responding to Criticism

**Number of Characters:** 4

**Character Descriptions:** Adair–a student
Linley–Adair's older brother
Mr. Taylor–Adair's father
Narrator

**Props:** Dinosaur model

**Scene Description:** Adair is building a dinosaur model for a school project. His brother and father are looking at it with him.

## Skill 36
# Responding to Criticism

*Script A*

ADAIR
What do you think? Does it look right?

LINLEY
It looks a little short-legged to me. I suggest making the legs longer so it looks more like the picture.

ADAIR
What do you think, Dad?

MR. TAYLOR
I agree with Linley, Adair. I suggest lengthening the legs, but not too much. You don't want it to look like it's walking on stilts. [Looks at the model more closely.] Another thing I see is that the teeth aren't quite right. [They all examine the teeth.]

LINLEY
I see what you mean. The teeth in the picture are pretty pointy. These are squared off at the bottom. [Points to the teeth on the model.]

ADAIR
I see what you mean about the legs. [Picks up the model.] Let me see those teeth again, too. [Examines the teeth more closely.] How can I make them more pointy?

MR. TAYLOR
I think you could just sharpen them a little bit. What do you think, Linley?

LINLEY
I agree. Adair, do you want to borrow my sharp artist knife?

ADAIR
Sure! That thing should make great points! Thanks, Linley. And would you help me make sure I don't get them too pointy?

*Continued on next page*

# Skill 36

# Responding to Criticism—*Continued*

| | |
|---|---|
| LINLEY | [Laughs.] **Yes. You don't want it to look like a snaggle-tooth tiger!** |
| NARRATOR | [Adair sharpens the teeth and lengthens the legs. Then she brings the model to Linley's room.] |
| ADAIR | **How does this look? Do you think I got them sharp enough?** |
| LINLEY | [Looks at the teeth.] **These look just right. It looks like the picture now, don't you think?** |
| NARRATOR | [Linley goes to get her father, who is in the living room.] |
| LINLEY | **Hey, Dad, you should see what a great job Adair did! Come see!** |
| MR. TAYLOR | [Comes in and looks at the model.] **Hey, this looks terrific, Adair. You did a nice job on the teeth and on the legs. Now it looks almost identical to the picture.** |
| ADAIR | **Thanks, Dad. Thanks, Linley. Your suggestions really helped me make it better.** |

*Skill 36*

# Responding to Criticism

**Number of Characters:** 4

**Character Descriptions:** Ms. Friedman–the soccer coach
Members of a soccer team:
- Da-Xia
- Oran
- Jana

**Scene Description:** The team has just finished a game, and Ms. Friedman is giving them pointers about how they played.

*Skill 36*

# Responding to Criticism

**Script B**

| | |
|---|---|
| Ms. Friedman | **Da-Xia, you did a great job on defense, but on offense, I need you to stay in your zone. It didn't hurt us today, but next week we'll have a tougher opponent.** |
| Da-Xia | [Smiles.] **OK, Coach. I'll work on staying in my zone.** |
| Ms. Friedman | **Oran, you need to remember to pass in both directions. You tend to pass to your right and not your left. That defender started to anticipate your passes.** |
| Oran | **I did that on purpose. I'm faster to my right, so I tried to pass that direction so I could follow up faster.** |
| Ms. Friedman | **I know you're faster off your right leg, but I still need you to pass in both directions. You had teammates open to your left several times, but you didn't even see them.** |
| Jana | **I was open twice, Oran.** |
| Oran | [Mumbles under his breath.] **I don't care what they say. I'm not changing it.** |
| Ms. Friedman | **I missed that, Oran. What did you say?** |
| Oran | **Nothing.** |
| Ms. Friedman | **OK. If you want to say something, say it so everyone can hear.** [Turns to Jana.] **Jana, you were right about being open. You could be more help, though, if you would wait a little bit to see what your defender is going to do. Then make your move. You'll get open more often if you fake them out.** |

*Continued on next page*

## Skill 36
# Responding to Criticism—Continued

JANA
**OK, Ms. Friedman.**

[Oran continues to grumble under his breath.]

MS. FRIEDMAN
**Oran, I can't hear what you're saying. . . .** [Oran quits grumbling, but he won't look at Ms. Friedman.] **OK, team, that's all for today. Go have fun!**

[Da-Xia, Oran, and Jana walk together.]

DA-XIA
**I like how Coach Friedman helps us with our game. I've got to remember to stay in my zone.**

JANA
**I agree; she's really good. She's right about faking out the defender, too. I'm going to work on that next week.**

ORAN
**She's always criticizing us! According to her, we can never do anything right. I'm sick of hearing what I did wrong.**

DA-XIA
**She's giving us helpful criticism, Oran. She's really trying to help us play better, that's all. If we listen to her, we will all learn something.**

ORAN
**I don't think so. I'm quitting!** [Walks away angrily.]

JANA
**I guess he doesn't know how to accept criticism.**

DA-XIA
**He'll never learn to play with that attitude. Ms. Friedman is just trying to help us play better. No coach will want him on the team if he won't listen to helpful criticism and learn from it.**

JANA
**You got that right!**

*Skill 37*

# Helping My Community

**Staging**

## Definition
Identifying the needs of my community and doing my part to help.

## Activities/Discussions

1. Lead a discussion of what *community* means, emphasizing the concept of a group with shared interests.

2. Ask students for examples of communities. List them on an overhead or on the board under these headings:
   - Family
   - Religion
   - Politics
   - Cultural background
   - Geographical location
   - Interest (e.g., weather, birds, collecting coins)
   - Profession

3. Discuss with students the idea of their school as a community and their class as a smaller community within the larger one. Have them identify the unique characteristics of their class.

---

## Alternative Settings

☐ **Home**—Your family has a suggestion box. What idea for helping your community would you put in it. How would you solve the need?

☐ **School**—Your school is beginning a peer-tutoring program. You believe you would be a good math tutor for younger students. Describe what you would do to get involved in the program.

☐ **Community**—Your local newspaper is sponsoring a citywide parks cleanup. Describe what you would do to participate.

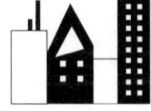

## Skill 37

# Helping My Community

**Number of Characters:** 3

**Character Descriptions:** Macy–a student
Wick–a student
Takuro–a student

**Props:** Newspaper; computer; calculator

**Scene Description:** Wick has found an article in the newspaper that announces a local pet adoption agency, The Haven, is sponsoring a 5-kilometer benefit walk. The three are discussing what they need to do to participate.

**Script A**

## Skill 37

# Helping My Community

MACY     **What do we need to do?**

WICK     [Reads from the newspaper article.] **"Help animals find homes. Volunteers can register either online or by calling The Haven at 445–8993." There's a website where we can register and get more information.**

TAKURO     **My dad showed me how to use a website to register. Let's try it.** [Types in the website.] **OK, here we go. Here's the link to register, and here's the link to print out the forms we use for the sponsors.**

MACY     **How many sponsors do we need to get?**

TAKURO     **It says we can get as many as we want, but you don't need a lot. That's good, because I'm not sure how many people I can get to sponsor me.**

WICK     **Are you kidding? All you have to do is get the phone numbers of your sister's friends. They'll all sponsor you. They'll think this is a great idea!** [Looks over Takuro's shoulder at the website.] **How much do we ask them to donate?**

TAKURO     **They suggest asking sponsors to donate a dollar per kilometer. That'd be $5 for each sponsor, but they can give whatever they want really.**

MACY     **Great! I'm going to ask everyone in my class to sponsor me. That'd be 29 people. How much is that?** [Calculates the figures.] **That'd be $145! Wow!**

*Continued on next page*

*Skill 37*

# Helping My Community—*Continued*

WICK — They probably won't all give you $5, though. Still, even if they gave you whatever they could, that'd be a lot! Every little bit helps, you know. We wouldn't want anyone to feel bad if they couldn't give $5.

TAKURO — No kidding! Who are you going to ask, Wick?

WICK — My parents know lots of people who love animals. I'm going to call them and ask them to sponsor me. But I'm going to ask them for more money per kilometer. They're adults; they have more money than kids do.

MACY — How much are you going to ask them for?

WICK — Do you think five dollars per kilometer is too much? That'd be $25 each.

TAKURO — Why don't you ask your parents? They'll know how much to ask for.

WICK — Good idea! So, what do we have to do to register? Can we do it all at once?

TAKURO — I don't think so. We can do it one at a time, though, and then print out the sponsor forms.

MACY — I'm really glad we're doing this. I like the idea of helping animals find homes.

TAKURO — Me, too. It's sure a good cause! I'm glad you saw this article, Wick.

## Skill 37

# Helping My Community

**Number of Characters:** 4

**Character Descriptions:** Baker–Katia's brother
Katia–Baker's sister
Zita–Katia and Baker's cousin
Wynn–Katia and Baker's cousin

**Scene Description:** Zita and Wynn and their parents are visiting Baker and Katia's family. Baker and Katia are telling Zita and Wynn about a community service project they participated in at their school.

## Skill 37

# Helping My Community

BAKER     Our school does a different community project for each grade. This year our grade worked on the Town Lake cleanup.

KATIA     Everyone in our grade wrote the Environmental Protection Agency telling them that fish farms might make the native fish sick and that they can damage the ocean.

ZITA     That sounds weird. How does that make any difference?

WYNN     I can see how cleaning up the lake would look better. But how does writing letters change anything?

KATIA     If students from all over the country wrote letters, people would pay attention.

WYNN     Who's going to pay attention to a bunch of kids?

BAKER     Well, the tuna companies sure did! Don't you remember? Kids from all over the world started to write letters asking them to stop catching dolphins in their nets. And you know what happened? The tuna companies changed how they caught tuna.

ZITA     I don't believe that! There's no way kids can change something like that!

KATIA     It's true! We did a dolphin-safe webquest and learned how they wrote millions of letters to senators and legislators.

WYNN     [Whistles.] **Wow! Really? You're not kidding us?**

*Continued on next page*

## Skill 37

# Helping My Community—Continued

| | |
|---|---|
| BAKER | She's not kidding you. |
| ZITA | I still don't believe it. It sounds too good to be true. |
| BAKER | Didn't you hear about how the school kids helped Keiko? |
| ZITA | You mean Keiko, the whale? |
| KATIA | Yes. In 1996, he went to the Oregon Coast Aquarium, and the people there helped him get well. Then, in 1998, he got airlifted to Iceland so he could be where he was born. Thousands of kids donated money to help pay for his trip. |
| WYNN | I was a little kid, but I remember that. I saw pictures of him in a big sling. And there were kids lining the road between the aquarium and the airport. |
| BAKER | Yeah, it was the middle of the night, and they all had flashlights and candles to help light the way. |
| ZITA | Big deal. |
| KATIA | It is a big deal! We kids can make a huge difference. You just have to get involved. Then you'll see. |
| WYNN | I might ask my teacher to start something like this. It seems like a really good idea. What do you think, Zita? Don't you think it's a good idea? |
| ZITA | I don't know. I'm not sure. |

# Appendix: Follow-Up Activities

**NOTE:** Enlist the assistance of school staff to help reinforce positive behaviors of students and do follow-up activities. This is especially important for students who may not have sufficient resources outside of school.

## Instructions for Activities

### Activity 1

*Follow-Up Activity 1* is to be completed as a homework assignment. Students role-play a social communication skill with an adult, which promotes transfer of the skill outside the classroom. You may wish to assign *Follow-Up Activity 1* more than once while you are teaching social skills. For each Follow-up activity, modify the language to meet your students' developmental levels.

Before the students use the Follow-Up Activity templates, have them add the following information:

- Current date
- Their name
- Social communication skill they will be role-playing
- The skill steps
- The due date
- The situation in which the skill will be role-played

After checking to make sure the appropriate information is on the sheet, sign the educator line.

# Scripting Junior

## Activity 2

The *Follow-Up Activity 2* template can be completed by students at any time while they are learning these social skills. Whether this activity is completed individually or by groups, help students choose a script that has particular relevance for the student(s). You may wish to assign *Follow-Up Activity 2* more than once while you are teaching social skills.

## Activity 3 and 4

*Follow-Up Activity 3* is for younger students or students who need more structure. *Follow-Up Activity 4* is for older students or students who need less structure. This activity is best done as a group, although it can be completed by individuals given appropriate guidance. You may wish to use more than one of these Follow-Up Activity assignments while you are teaching social skills.

*Appendix: Follow-Up Activities*

# Follow-Up Activity 1

Date:_____

**Dear Parent or Guardian of** _____,

We are learning about the **social communication skill:** _____

This skill can be broken down into the following **skill steps:** _____
_____
_____
_____

Please role-play (practice) the situation described below with your son/daughter, or arrange for her or him to practice with another responsible adult. After completing the role-play, sign your name at the bottom of this sheet. This activity sheet needs to be returned by _____.

---

**Situation:**
_____
_____
_____
_____

---

By practicing this social communication skill at home, your child will be more likely to use the skill outside of the classroom setting.

Thank you for your assistance.

Sincerely,

_____
               *Educator*

*Parent/Guardian Signature* _____

From *Scripting: Social Communication for Adolescents* (p.15), by P. Mayo and P. Waldo, 1994, Eau Claire, WI: Thinking Publications. © 1994, by Thinking Publications. Adapted with permission.

Scripting Junior

## Follow-Up Activity 2

Date: _____

Name(s): _____

**Directions:** Choose the script for a social skill you're working on. Read through it (Or have someone read it to you). Then, answer these questions.

1. What social skill is used in this script? _____
   _____

2. Why is this social skill important to learn? _____
   _____

3. Which person (or persons) in the script used this social skill? _____
   _____

   Did he or she use it correctly? _____

4. How do you think learning this social skill will help you in school? _____
   _____
   _____

5. How might learning this social skill help you outside school? _____
   _____
   _____

6. List three situations in which you have used, or might need to use, this social skill.
   _____
   _____
   _____

From *Scripting: Social Communication for Adolescents* (p.15), by P. Mayo and P. Waldo, 1994, Eau Claire, WI: Thinking Publications. © 1994 by Thinking Publications. Adapted with permission.

*Appendix: Follow-Up Activities*

# Follow-Up Activity 3

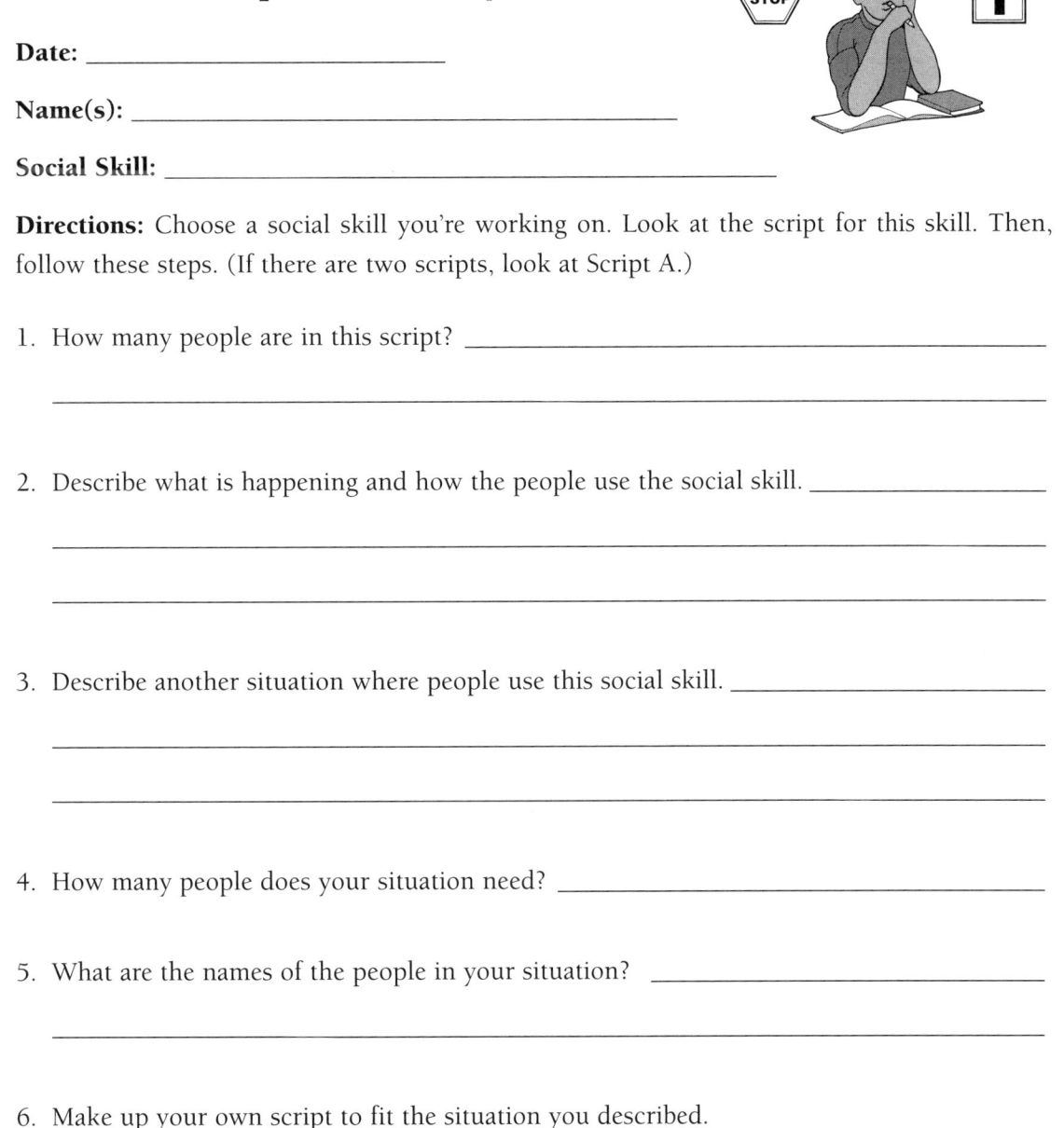

**Date:** _____

**Name(s):** _____

**Social Skill:** _____

**Directions:** Choose a social skill you're working on. Look at the script for this skill. Then, follow these steps. (If there are two scripts, look at Script A.)

1. How many people are in this script? _____
   _____

2. Describe what is happening and how the people use the social skill. _____
   _____
   _____

3. Describe another situation where people use this social skill. _____
   _____
   _____

4. How many people does your situation need? _____

5. What are the names of the people in your situation? _____
   _____

6. Make up your own script to fit the situation you described.

*Scripting Junior* © 2004 Thinking Publications

Scripting Junior

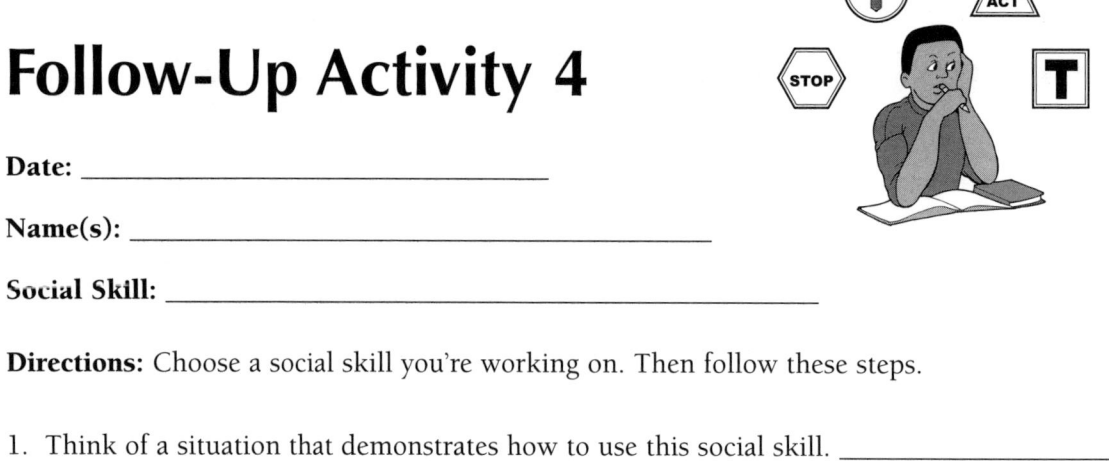

# Follow-Up Activity 4

**Date:** _____

**Name(s):** _____

**Social Skill:** _____

**Directions:** Choose a social skill you're working on. Then follow these steps.

1. Think of a situation that demonstrates how to use this social skill. _____
   _____
   _____
   _____
   _____

2. Decide how many characters you need for your script. _____

3. Name your characters. _____
   _____
   _____
   _____

4. Using the situation you've described, write a script that demonstrates how to use this social skill.

# References

Elliott, S., & Gresham, F. (1991). *Social skills intervention guide: Practical strategies for social skill training.* Circle Pines, MN: American Guidance Service.

Gajewski, N., Hirn, P., & Mayo, P. (1993). *Social star: General interaction skills (Book 1).* Greenville, SC: Super Duper® Publications.

Gajewski, N., Hirn, P., & Mayo, P. (1994). *Social star: Peer interaction skills (Book 2).* Greenville, SC: Super Duper® Publications.

Gajewski, N., Hirn, P., & Mayo, P. (1996). *Social star: Conflict resolution and community interaction skills (Book 3).* Greenville, SC: Super Duper® Publications.

Goldstein, A., Sprafkin, R., Gershaw, N., & Klein, P. (1980). *Skillstreaming the adolescent: A structured learning approach to teaching prosocial skills.* Champaign, IL: Research Press.

Madden, N., & Slavin, R. (1983). Mainstreaming students with mild handicaps: Academic and social outcomes. *Journal of Education Research, 53,* 519–569.

Mayo, P., & Waldo, P. (1994). *Scripting: Social communication for adolescents* (2nd ed.). Greenville, SC: Super Duper® Publications.

McGinnis, E., Goldstein, A., Sprafkin, R., & Gershaw, N. (1984). *Skillstreaming the elementary school child: A guide for teaching prosocial skills.* Champaign, IL: Research Press.

Merriam-Webster.com. Definition of "social." Retrieved 8/22/03 from http://www.merriam-webster.com/cgi-bin/dictionary.

Paul, R. (2001). *Language disorders from infancy through adolescence: Assessment and intervention* (2nd ed.). St. Louis, MO: Mosby.

Polloway, E., Miller, L., & Smith, T. E. C. (2004). *Language instruction for students with disabilities* (3rd ed.). Denver, CO: Love Publishing.

Strain, P., Odom, S., & McConnell, S. (1984). Promoting social reciprocity of exceptional children: Identification of target behavior selection and intervention. *Remedial and Special Education, 5,* 21–28.